How My Ancestors Drink Whiskey:

Essays, Poems & Rituals on Growing
through Uncertainty.

Joi Donaldson

ISBN: 978-0-578-62455-6
Publisher: The Joi Element Publishing

To my maternal ancestral squad:

Amorette Scott

Mamie Lockett

Gayle Scott

To my Intellectual Ancestors:

Maya Angelou

James Baldwin

Josephine Baker

Zora Neale Hurston

Langston Hughes

Lorraine Hansberry

Ida B. Wells

Toni Morrison

I write because of you. I write for you.

I'm worried this book isn't long enough
I'm worried that the beats of these words and of my heart
sound just like humming
And if you're not paying attention, you'll miss it

I'm not going to deny myself these pangs
The worries of me having all the things to say

Whoever finds this book was meant to
And the words will sing loud and strong
They will ring back years later in a conversation
About that book you once read
Dog-eared and slept beside
And then I will know

This book was long enough.

How do you close the door on a fresh piercing?

How do you race to get the last iced Thai tea at Broad Appetit?

How do you cope after waking up on a Tuesday to meet it on your chest, mouth tight and lips tucked, telling you to "take yo ass back to sleep?"

How do you give up on church?

How do you take God out of the box, packing peanuts and all?

How do you smile? While having a vulva? While being Black? And being told to choose?

How do you love a kid who reminds you of both their cool and the marks on your body that got them here?

How, with no respect to the code, say "bitch, fuck this and fuck yall?"

How.

How.

How has been the reason I've allowed my boundaries to go unseen. How has been the driving force behind my sleepless nights. How is what burrows deep inside me when I cannot and do not understand.

How.

The word has haunted my life. How do I live? How do I pay these bills? How do I stop suffering? In positing this particular adverb across the landscape of these slivers of my life, I am actively coming to terms with not knowing all the answers while also not negating the ones I do. The weight of uncertainty brings brakes to our feet. We are halted in our tracks while progressing at a heavy clip. Uncertainty births the hows.

With this book with the lessons still fresh, I write in real-time as the coast clears on some of the hows in my life. The essays and poems within are followed by words of wisdom to hopefully help answer some of the future hows.

Preface

How my ancestors drink whiskey

I'm from Virginia. Richmond to be clear. Southside to be exact. Blackwell & Broad Rock to be specific. I find my roots in the capital of the confederacy. The now-evolving epicenter of mostly one-sided, one-hued creativity known to outsiders as RVA. I'm from a city that taught me looking deeper is a means to survival. That playing on the surface will at least get you embarrassed and, at most, get you killed. My ancestry runs as far south as the Carolinas and as far north as Maryland. Tracing footsteps both physical and metaphysical led me to learn how to commune with those higher than I. My ancestors have their own designated altar in my dining room. A big photo of my maternal grandmother sits in the middle, underneath her a scrap of brown paper holding her mother's name. My great-grandmother passed 15 years before I was born but she comes to me in visions as a large blackbird. She's protective, stoic and loving. My grandmother, barely five feet, was a force in her younger years. I wish I would've known more of that side of her growing up. I got to know the worn, tired yet resilient side of her and with that, I am still grateful. My maternal aunt and cousin are also written out on a piece of brown paper. They sit nestled by the window, facing the sun as it sets and the moon as it rises. They show their happiness and displeasure. They speak when I walk by them. They remind me to walk tall, pray, ask for protection, give them what they desire.

Recently, I put my father on my altar. He died when I was 20, him and my grandmother going on to glory two months apart. The older I got, the farther he pulled away. So much so that at the beginnings of this part of my journey, while conducting a cord-cutting ritual, he said I should cut ties with him too. From that moment, I etched him out of my life. Still, for years I would smell him in the air, wafts of old cologne. I asked a reader whether I was venerating the right ancestors. She told me no. I was dejected. Then we went deeper. Because my specific roots are so jagged - due to abuse, secrecy, betrayal - I don't have a solid line to carve. I know no one ancestrally on my dad's side but him and in his waking life, he made me out to be the world's worst kept secret. The ties that bind, bind us tightest. And what happens in this family is none of your concern.

"There's your problem - you've cut yourself off from your father", the reader said.

No, he cut himself off from me.

"There's so much healing that needs to happen here. Maybe this is the start."

I don't want this to be the start.

"This is why it hurts, Joi".

I fell silent.

"I know this is a tall order to ask. But no one else can do this but you."

It's no wonder why my mother drank her spirit to near-death.

I know nothing of Whiskey, or any alcohol for that matter. I choose not to drink due to my surroundings growing up. Now, as I lay in my living room at the feet of their altar, I'm working through how to do this. How to make room for someone who left me out in the cold.

It's true you can't heal *for* others, as in do the dirty work while they reap the benefits. At least not cleanly. Not without resentment. Within the work of ancestor veneration, our healing affects us as well as those above us. So, in a way, we *are* healing for others. The big ask is are you willing to sacrifice, knowing that some prayers may go unanswered? Some old processes may resurface. Some hard-fought battles may end in pyrrhic victories. This road isn't for everyone. Some may never experience teaching their ancestors how to love them the way they need it, how to love themselves and how to be loved. But for the few that are experiencing this, know that nights wailing in front of your altar are valid. That going days without speaking are a possibility. That being utterly confused is the norm. That forgiveness is sometimes given, then reneged. That boundaries and sacrifice go hand-in-hand. That one day, it'll all make some kind of sense.

The Hows have roots

How to talk to your ancestors

I told my ancestors that I needed them to love me loudly across dimensions as they did not show me love while here on earth. I needed them to show me every day how much they love me. I laid at my altar and cried tears I didn't know I had stored for this feeling. I was empty; going through the motions of prettying up a space for people who just didn't have the capacity to show up in ways I needed. Sometimes, I didn't either. Some of the lost language was due to safety. Protection. They'd been hurt by showing love so not showing it *must* be the solution. It no longer mattered the person, place or identity - no one would know love here again. In beginning my veneration work of my ancestors, I've had to show up in my humanity while also acknowledging theirs. I have to be as naked, covered, awake, quiet as I can be. I stopped performing once I approached them wounded, open and as my full self.

Do not be afraid to or be guilted out of setting boundaries with your folk. Informing them and coming to them in your fullness packs power. Even if you're someone being led to heal your lineage, you're not a puppet. Let your folks know. We're all grown here and acknowledgment of limits is not blasphemous or disrespectful. They love you. They know you because, in this life, they are you. And they understand.

If you're just starting your ancestral work and veneration, here are a few tips to form a healthy routine:

You ever caught a whisper behind your ear? The smell of food, perfume, cologne that isn't present? Cravings for food you don't normally eat? That is most likely an ancestor trying to connect with you. How are your ancestors? Ask around your family about how your grandparents, aunts and uncles and extended family were before you came along. Ask about their temperaments, their achievements, their failures. Decide who you'd like to connect with while remaining open. Some ancestors choose us; don't block them simply because you don't recognize them. That's not to say don't use discretion. Be diligent and mindful of who you connect with.

~ Set up an ancestor altar in the best spot in your home for daily engagement (try to avoid your bedroom if you can). Make sure the altar is lifted off the ground with a flat surface wide enough to hold the following items:

a clear glass of water to serve as a portal

a light blue or white candle to light and guide the way

photos of your ancestors. Make sure to only use those who have passed and not photos of anyone still living.

if you don't have photos, write their names on a piece of paper. If you'd like, place the name paper in a picture frame

their favorite foods/drinks/vices.

~ Engage. Engage daily. Don't leave them in the corner to be memorialized but not spoken to. I'm guilty of this and as I write this, my grandmother is pulling at me to acknowledge I must do a better job. Ancestors seek to help us, but just as beings on this earthly plane get rung out and flung to the side, they feel the same impact of thanklessness. Let's be mindful to thank and bless them every day just for who they are in our lives. Start small: some candy, fruit, nips of alcohol, tea, water, ancestor and real money are just a few items to always have handy. If you chef it up on the regular, make them a plate as well. Just be easy on the salt for their offering.

~ Sacrifice is a worthy cause when engaging with your Egun, or ancestors. I admit I was wary of this. Mainly because for much of my life, sacrifice meant death. Of my mind, my desires, my soul. I expressed that to my ancestors as to circumvent any tings of apprehension from me. I asked them to be soft and patient with me as sacrifice takes on a new definition. I give thanks that they have listened and are working with me. Ancestors want what they want. You may not eat meat *raises hand* and they want pork sausages. You may not drink *points to self* and they want beer. Make your boundaries clear and adjust when and where *you* feel led. They won't curse your existence. Again, they know you and love you. They are working tirelessly on the other side to provide for us. A sacrifice is giving them what they desire within the bounds of what's possible for you.

~ Walk by their altar every day and tell them you love them. Ask for their insight, protection, wisdom. Give them a plate of the last thing you cooked. Ask that ancestors of love, light and power come forward only. Not every ancestor was/is good with some kicking up dust even in the afterlife. Ask that a strong shield be woven around you. That all for you be for your highest and greatest good. Name your squad: I call mine my Divine Tribe.

Our ancestors stand in the gap for us on the other side. They lay down maps at our feet. They peek through the veil to help us in ways mortals can't or won't. They ask us to honor the earth, their legacies, their wins and losses. Ancestors ask us to pick up the banner where they left off or give us the blessing to start anew. They seek the sky when we can't bear our eyes towards Heaven. They call out our shit and desire the best for and from us. They see what we can't and work to steer us clear. This is how we speak to them:

By calling them by name.

By honoring their altars and sacred spaces.

By acknowledging their efforts.

By slowing down to listen to them.

By pouring libations.

By seeing them in nature.

Pay attention to your dreams. To certain smells in the air. To coincidences. To voices so close in the silence.

The ancestors are present.

How to be accidentally inspiring

I don't always know how I got here. Why I chose to incarnate in this space, at this time, in this body, with these problems, on that day. I wonder if I made the right choice. If I felt compelled to be here because I knew I would make a difference or was a deal reached that I will only make good on when I leave this plane. At any rate, I'm grateful to be here.

I want to make sure I am speaking what is deepest inside me. I tend to pull at the surface for fear that my words carry too much weight. No one asked to hold something so heavy so I try to make myself light; to appease and abandon what I'm actually trying to get across. At times, I even fool myself into thinking what I'm performing is actually intentional. I know that I have more; I just don't want to show. Or I'm afraid/ashamed to show it. I dance along the line of deliberate delusion. In purposeful melancholy. Then get angry with the world when I'm not understood. I try to think of who I'm meant to be and be that. Skip a few letters and lessons to get to the meat and hope for the best on the final exam. I stand as a moving symbol of hope, and dogs don't bark at parked symbols. I wonder why I continue to raise these banners. Why I would make my home as an infirmary for the wounded. Why I understand chaos and sit so uncomfortably in peace. Who said my life had to be a puzzle? My sanity a thread with which I keep stitching together meaning? I forget to wash me off at night: the painted face on top of the mask on top of a woman carrying the world. When I remember, I fill the sink, pour myself in, break against the bowl, shaking away as much dirt I can while holding on to some because who can be too clean. I ring myself out, toss me over the shower rod and meet myself again in the morning.

I don't know how to be fully at rest. I don't know how to live without at least one knot in my stomach. Without at least one panic attack. Without at least one depressive episode.

"But girl, you just got your shit *together*."

I've been on a purge. Heavy into therapy. Learning and unlearning my codependent sensibilities. Having the string pulled and watching the patchwork of my life fall apart. I can run to catch all the remnants if I want - it'll never go back together as once before. And I'm better for it. Still, that doesn't mean it doesn't HURT to watch all that work hit the ground.

In tearing down the monuments to shame, guilt and light&love, I've found me buried beneath the rubble. To think my livelihood depended upon hoping someone would find me and nurse me back to health. Yet, I found me and had no idea what to do. So I started over.

Some words on starting over

#1. Decide why you need to. Are you starting over because it feels right or because it's expected? Decide what starting over holds for you. This isn't simply clearing out your Instagram page. This can be anywhere from a semi-redux to a full overhaul. Your why matters here because it determines how deep you will go. Outside forces determining your level of commitment will surely derail your confidence and access to the fullness of self you're attempting to reach. Make your why yours and yours alone.

#2. Determine what's missing. There's a hollowness that comes with self-discovery. Identities and hard-kept ideologies begin to fall away, leaving an open space you aren't readily prepared to fill. And that's okay. You'll hear me say that a lot in this book. Name the missing parts. Whether writing them out or speaking them out loud, call out what's gone missing. This will help you have a deeper understanding of what's gone and why it had to leave.

#3. Learn the good in being uncomfortable. Many of us lived our lives laying on nails. We were told, or told ourselves that this was good enough. As the adage goes, we'll move once the pain gets to be too much. We've learned how to be uncomfortable out of necessity. To not make a fuss. To grin and bear it. I definitely did. Yet growth begets discomfort. It's a weird mindfuck to line up the past with the present - the traumatic with the thriving - to find the same feeling can benefit one and collapse the other. It calls for an updated stream of thought that welcomes that which once caused distress. The things that make you uncomfortable are there to be surmounted, not feared. The level of *You* you've been seeking is always on the other side of discomfort.

One second at a time
In every new breath
With a clean mirror

How to cut at the roots

I must care enough to cut it all off and begin again.

Three people turned down my asking to make my pixie
cut dreams come true. One considered it a dishonor, one
swore we could be healthy together and the last never
returned my calls. At first, it was funny - leaping over flat
irons to find someone brave enough with a pair of shears.
Then the reality of why so much dodging began to set in:
I'm a Black girl with long curly hair that can't be
pinpointed directly to a specific ancestry. I am yet a
unicorn. So why would I cut my horn to spite my face? I
struggle with why we cherish our hair. My mother jokes
when I was born my hair was longer than me. I've never
lived that down. I watched my grandmother lose more
and more light in her eyes as cancer plucked nearly every
strand from her head. I've witnessed the light return to a
friend in her bald glory during remission. I've pulled out
clumps of my own during wash day due to stress and
protein deficiencies. Some days I wonder who controls
who and why we care so much. "Bald-head bitch" is one of
our first insults. But who taught us that bald or short hair
is specifically Black woman leprosy? We unconsciously
dole out hate based on beauty standards that aren't even
ours. "Why would/did you cut it??", I'm asked now.
"Because it died" is always my answer. It's the true
answer. And then understanding is applied.

I've had to envision myself in the light I'm in now. My crown does not stretch to Heaven as it once did but I'm no less royalty. I'm no less angelic.

My particular brand of natural hair has always been a battleground for me long before I was aware. Within my strands laid power and animosity, strength and fragility, gainful employment and reprimands. In losing so much, I've gained an understanding of myself as defined as my multi-textured curls. I am loose and tight, bound and strong, moisturized and never dry. I grow when I am nourished and cared for by my own hands. A big chop continues to grow where the roots were severed. Long live the kinks.

Some words on doing the thing scared:

#1. Remind yourself who you're doing it for. If you need reminding, it's you. Outside of medical reasons, the only reason to swap up styles is to make yourself glow. Partners come and go, what's in vogue waxes and wanes. But if the style is yours to claim and it makes you feel otherworldly, go for it.

#2. Remind yourself why you're doing it. Remember your because. It can be one word or paragraphs of feelings. It can be to release yourself from the ickiness of a bad breakup or to cut off dying things like I had to do. Draw your because from within, not based on anyone's outside commentary. And speaking of such...

#3. Other peoples' worries are not your worries. The disheartening fact is most women, specifically Black and WOC, are warned to not cut their hair because the domineering patriarchy wards against it. The shame to no longer be viewed as fuckable to a mass of men who see you as property or something to conquer. Their fears are not yours. Their worries, not yours. Cut away, sib and get the freedom you deserve.

How to let go

I've been in love multiple times. Times in love when I lost
my whole self - a self I wasn't fully invested in. I told
myself if I loved them hard, sweet, long enough, they
would return that love tenfold. It never happened. I had
that same thought towards my parents and any person I
laid down my body for. The love, labor and loyalty were
never returned. So, after years of wiping mud and tears
from my face, I got sick of sitting in my own shit. I noticed
that as I poured into others, it left me dry and nearly
comatose. It was awkward and unfamiliar, but I began to
turn away from helping others to my detriment. I began to
water myself as my own garden. And, so so slowly, I
began to let them go. I still have moments where I play
out scenarios in the shower. Moments where I wake up
screaming and angry. Moments I lament why my kindness
was sent through the wringer. I still don't have clear
answers. I just know I can't continue to carry these loads.
So how does one start? How do you begin letting people,
scenarios, lost love, situations, places, old dreams go?
One letter at a time.

Some words on letting go

#1. Acknowledge the pain. It's there. You feel it every day. It's a weight on your chest; a knot in your throat. It causes nightmares, "irrational" behaviors and copious amounts of precaution. Every last bit of that is valid. It's real. It happened to you. Let it be real in your life without allowing it to consume you. Acknowledge its presence but don't bid it to stay with you. Shit like pain likes to sneak up and the next thing you know it's moved in eating all your food. Put it on notice before it goes too far.

#2. Find a bomb ass therapist and sort some shit out. No, you don't have to go through this alone. No, therapy is not just for white people. Yes, it is that serious.

#3. Don't allow anyone to minimize your journey. Some of us have gone through things most can't fathom. Yet, it takes one person to tell us that someone has it way worse than we do and we begin to call into question our own lives. Yes, every bit of your story matters. The things done against you and the things you brought to your doorstep. The things you didn't mean to bring to pass and the things set out to pass you by. It all matters. And no one person's pain invalidates another.

How to have Imposter Syndrome

Sounds like
Envisioning the very best version of me
The one where my badassery is untethered
The one where I walk slowly in a dress of all colors
Cascading. Flowing.
My hair is in a braided bun
Covered in piercings and tattoos
Manipulating blue orbs of light in my palms
My face is dotted in war paint
I am in my own pace, Shuri
I am sure of it
Striking fear in any who step across my path with evil
intentions
Where I move mountains with ease
And the voice goes
"What if they don't believe me?"
"Because I don't always believe me. I can't truly be this
level of warrior. How?"
"It's not nice. You're being too much. You have to let them
win. It's the respectable, polite thing to do"
"Lay down your weapon. Die. In honor. In polite remorse.
For the sake of the feelings of your murderer. That's how
you gain true love"
"So you don't want to die? You're selfish. You're a coward.
You're in no way this full of wonder."
"Drink the poison, the guilt. That's the only way to absolve
yourself of the sin of thinking you could be any more than
this"

"Pay for this with the blood of overthinking, the loss of sleep, the meandering monotony of your mediocrity. You ain't shit. Stop trying to be it."

Wounded warrior on the battlefield of life

Some words on acknowledging Imposter Syndrome

#1: Catch it as it's happening. That loud voice in the back of your head telling you that all of this was a mistake. That you will be found out soon to be a fraud because you have no letters behind your name. It stems from fear. The best way to begin to stop the cycle is notice when it's happening. Right before you're about to deny your greatness, it will begin to speak for you. Do a self-check and see what it's causing you. Duress? Stress? Pain? Inability to speak? Darting eyes? Self-deprecation? Avoidance? All of these are signs I.S. is attempting to butt in. Do some gentle self-talk by reminding yourself you've done the work to be where you are. Your accomplishments and the praise you receive are accurate and valid.

#2. Some of the people we admire struggle too. Most people experience Imposter Syndrome while doing things they love, especially if they're naturally good at them. Imposter Syndrome makes a habit out of causing you to isolate yourself out of fear of being "found out". Let yourself be found: found doing the thing you excel at, the work you're passionate about, the art you love. Because no one does it like you.

#3. It's as much of a mental condition as it is a societal one. If we can't explain it, we question it. If we can't do it, it must be impossible. If anyone succeeds, they must have a secret weapon or are cheating. That's how most people view a select few that are doing their thing seemingly unhindered, no thought to the sleepless nights, lost friendships or money spent to achieve those wins. It's how resentment seeps into admiration and becomes hate. That's not your fault or anything you are required to answer for. How you succeed in this world is between you, your creator and the ancestors. Don't apologize for being good at something because it makes others uncomfortable. Let 'em be mad.

How to make it through Damascus

I remember coming back to life. I was about 3 or 4 and I
was being resuscitated after sneaking into the big kid
pool. I remember going under - seeing my last sights
before it all went dark. I woke up surrounded by bodies
and water spouting from my mouth. A few years later I
saw Heaven. I walked around looking like a 90s alt kid's
fantasy: hair in claw clips, purple long sleeve shirt and
baggy black cargo pants with deep pockets. I flew into a
cloud and walked around until I found the throne. On that
throne sat a face I couldn't see. I think I asked a question
but woke up before I had my answer. I told my mother and
she told her friends.

"Was He Black?"

My relationship with God up to this point has been like a
home that has a gaping hole where the living room used
to be. We're like the two you ship but keep missing each
other. I always felt I was missing pieces from my higher
self and my Creator but was always told tradition is better.
I was raised Baptist. I sang in the Children & Youth Choir,
found a steady alto, praised danced. I hit all the marks yet
nothing really satisfied my thirst for understanding.

I remember wondering why God seemed to hate me. Why
hearing Their voice was like listening for a muddled echo
and how I was such a fuck-up that I couldn't listen
correctly. I recall being numb in church, screaming in my
head why did they take my grandmother, how could they

allow Trump to win, why didn't they stop the person who molested me, why did they let me think I was at fault? Most of my thought process was a broken record of prayers asking what did I do wrong. I would pray against something and what I feared most would happen anyway. I blamed myself. What were they trying to prove? Why wouldn't they just let me know what's going on instead of expecting to me just "get it". WHAT IS THERE TO GET? In July 2016, I held my first protest march for Philando Castile. The next day on the highway back from a photo shoot in Maryland, my car broke down and never restarted. My pastor told me the devil doesn't bark at parked cars. We all know how hellish 2016 was. We lost so many greats. My high school basketball coach died by suicide. And I tearfully wandered around Richmond trying to understand it all. On the edge of Carytown stood a metaphysical store called the Aquarian. It's white as hell but few options are available in big R Religious Richmond. I'd always been curious but my Baptist thinking pushed me away. That particular day, I felt called there. As I stepped off the bus, I felt a push towards the building. I stepped in not knowing what to expect. My very first reading wasn't that great. In truth, all I remember is her telling me she saw the moon in me. My second reading with a new reader made me a believer. Upon sitting down after having a worrisome conversation about where my life and businesses are going, he looks at me and says, "girl what are you worried about? You better go help these girls and women!". By that point, I hadn't said my name. That changed my life.

On March 4th 2017, I had my road to Damascus moment by way of a painful breakup that knocked the breath out of me. The best way I can describe this moment is the eerily calm stillness right before an explosion. But instead, your tower *implodes*, leaving you deafened and shattered. That was my first time hearing Spirit clearly, as if they were sitting right next to me. I remember everything around me moving in slow motion. My tears felt like glass. The reimagining of a car crash, the day I drowned and was resuscitated as a kid, the colors navy blue and purple surrounding me. I have going 45 mph down a two-lane road. "You can hear me now," they said, ironically as I drove past my church home. Most of the words are a memory but the tactile feel of that moment remains.

I lived my life testing every time I heard God, refusing to believe the first time was the truth. I would ask over and over to be sure. I still do that, especially in trying times. Once I screamed at heaven that the lesson was too heavy; that the squeezing wasn't producing a diamond but instead causing irreversible pain. I left that prayer soaking wet and choking. In the calm as the smoke settled, I heard "I'm sorry. We've been pushing you too hard. We want the best for you and sometimes we forget, you're still human". I stood still. Did Heaven, my Divine Tribe, just apologize to *me?* Did my "take this cup from me!" prayer take root? I guess so. I've heard a couple more sorrys since then. I've said them too.

Recently I've gotten angry again. Calling God to carpet demanding an audience with them. I listed things I saw were wrong:

"How could you put Job through all those trials for basically a pissing contest? How could you put his life and sanity on the line just to say 'I told you so?'"

"Does our humanity matter? We aren't pawns. We're hurting in this game too."

My therapist once said Old Testament God was an asshole. He was irrational, egotistical, reactionary. He didn't truly know pain until he lost someone he cared for, then the blurry vision surrounding his creations become clear. I read a piece about Job where God told him those that said he couldn't be mad and question him were wrong. He was right; God was being irrational, God was causing hurt and Job apologized for his anger when he didn't have to. I sat on the train during my commute reading over that article. I read over and over again the part where righteous, biting anger can actually forge a deeper connection. I wasn't there yet; I needed God to know I was in pain. Why I was being distant because I already felt neglected, especially in the face of trying my best to do the right things. Do you not see me where I am, God, or is this still not good enough? I played with the idea of fully walking away. Of becoming cold and bitter and denouncing. How would my life look after? Would I recognize me? Would it make life better or worse? At this point, I'm not ready to let go, even though the hand I hold ushers in both my glory and abuse. And I wonder if to endure one for the hope of the other is even worth the trouble.

There are good days. Hearing Spirit at times is like the song of a Tibetan bowl. They whistle, they ring. They knock inside me. They lead and push. The one part I have trouble with it is when I don't hear them. There is where I'm afraid to move. A nudge follows and I'm reminded to trust my intuition. Trust what's been trusted. Trust what's already been shown. Feet off the ground now.

Some words on crises of faith

#1. Redefining home. As I touched on in the essay, I've always struggled with the story of Job and how God can just do a thing and expect everyone else to be on board. One of the best recounts I've read unpacking the story of Job was through the lens of Job's anger and him having every right to be mad[1]. The author posited that those telling him not to question or be angry were actually those with the biggest potential to cause him to slip. As I continue to unpack my religious upbringing, walking away from organized religion was the part I struggled with most. Because now I have no home, at least that's what I told myself. I wasn't so much straddling a fence as I was questioning what the fence was protecting. In doing that, the checkbox I had for God no longer checked out. How does one go about redefining home? Begin viewing home as bigger. I was conditioned to think on some shack shit when I'm really wired for acres. Place God in a bigger space and realize that God can inhabit any and everything. God isn't a gender. I took God out of the binary and put Them where they made sense for me. That's not blasphemous. Because if God is meeting us where we are, I'm right where I'm supposed to be.

---

[1] "Get angry with God: Job did | Tanya Marlow - Thorns and Gold." 27 Jun. 2012, https://tanyamarlow.com/get-angry-at-god-job-did-is-it-a-sin-to-be-angry-with-god-pt-ii/. Accessed 30 Oct. 2019.

#2. Having a crisis doesn't mean you've lost faith. I've discovered that Spirit speaks to me in spurts. It does this really annoying thing where it tells me the worst possible thing first when I least expect it and seemingly disappears when I have additional questions, i.e. wtf does that mean?! The usual reaction (the one I was raised with) is either to deny or react, neither of which brought any understanding. I had a deep crisis in early 2018 where everything I believed to be true collapsed. No one knew how to answer my questions and nothing I was experiencing added up to what was revealed to me years prior. Later that year, after all my gnashing, tearing and crying, my therapist said this: "just because we have the right map doesn't mean all involved will follow. You didn't hear wrong, people stepped out of destiny and now you're experiencing plan B. And that's okay". It wasn't the answer I was expecting but it was the answer I needed after 10 months of questioning. My crisis of faith took my faith to places I never imagined it could go. In doing so, it set my faith on a more solid ground than I knew before.

#3. Destiny and free will go hand-and-hand. Things can be revealed that make absolute total sense and fill you with joy. They can be answered prayers or promised restoration. That does not mean everyone will be on board. The partner of your dreams may manifest your downfall. The job you prayed for may cause you to crumble. The things destined to us don't follow a concrete plan and the moment we settle into that fact, the less attachment we have to the outcome. I'm a seer. I've had the gift of sight since I was a kid. I would see events and happenings before they took place, with outcomes and expectations usually the opposite of belief. I ran from this gift once I realized what it was because it was too heavy. Also, because people have an uncanny way of screwing things up, myself included, I didn't want that metaphysical smoke. I've seen so much that has come to pass and so much that hasn't. Not holding on so tightly to a certain outcome has helped me understand and work with this gift more fluidly. It's not always easy and what we want can oftentimes circumvent common sense, but learning how to release attachment to what we want creates room for more understanding.

How to self-care

Deep condition

Throw away

Give away

Purge/heave/release

Honor your past

Live in your present

Unlearn how to survive

Unlearn religion

Relearn how to pray

Understand your connection to spirit

Rearrange your altars

Update your vision board

Block/delete/report

Do not disturb mode

Masturbate & allow yourself full orgasms

Light that candle

Have a warm conversation

Ugly cry

Loud ugly laugh

Read

Don't read

Finish that thing

Don't finish that thing

Get up

Lay down

Stay in one space as long as you need to

Clean your social media and IRL friend lists

Respect your opinions

Give yourself grace, time and space

Flesh out boundaries and stick to them

Redecorate

Sweep/vacuum underneath your bed

Daydream

Twerk in the mirror

Protect yourself

Forgive yourself

Learn something new

Replay something old + do it better

Stay in some pain to recognize how it feels

Vow to never hurt like that again

How to obsess over Thai Tea

On Sunday, June 25th, 2017, on the cusp of Leslie Jones hosting the BET Awards and flying down the highway from an overnight stay in Maryland, I drank a watered-down iced Thai tea that ruined my whole vibe. Take also into account the owner staring me down until I stared back at her. Oh casual racism, you do know the right marks to hit. I left that place after experiencing what felt like a double hate crime to head home to catch the awards. Ironically, the best, most authentic Thai tea I've ever had was at a roadside Thai diner in iTsNoThAtEiTsHeRiTaGe, South Carolina. I was on vacation visiting friends in Georgia and stopped to grab some food on the way back to Virginia. I introduced the whole table to this sweet and tangy sensation that sets your face on a hot, Southern day towards the sun. I had 3 glasses because what's a sugar crash?

On Yelp, I confidently go by the moniker Foodie with the Fade. Because why not. My hair has since grown out, but my love for alliteration and fun internet names remains. My love of food and trying new things began in middle school when I was up at an ungodly hour casually nursing an episode of insomnia. I had seen peeks of the channel when my grandmother was awake and flipping past the guide. "BAM!" a loud chorus swelled from the living room tv that sat nestled on top of a bigger, broken, older tv. The same tv that kept the volume in the teens as to not wake the house. The jazz band played as this chef parlayed with 4 or 5 pans and griddles. Ramekins filled with spices lined the crescent-shaped bar where guests and chosen audience members gathered. The entire set was multicultural, something I noticed before I knew what I meant. Have you ever realized something was meant to be in real-time? Emeril Lagasse became my reason to live. I'd never seen food showcased so beautifully with an appreciation for its roots and culture. From that night and well into this present moment, Food Network, Cooking Channel and Viceland cooking shows are mainstays in my self-care routine. Alton Brown and *Good Eats* was and still is appointment tv and my absolute fave. The reload is even better, with Alton chastising his former self like a food-obsessed Doc careening back into time. *Bong Appetit* is fascinating. I'm no smoker (CBD is bae), but the dishes created with Cannabis makes me want to partake. Also, I just love the word *terpenes*. *F*ck That's Delicious*, even for a short while, satisfies both my wanderlust and curated curiosities. Carla Hall, Marcus Samuelsson and Alex Guarnaschelli are the G.O.A.T.s. *MasterChef* gives me a special kind of welcomed anxiety. *Nailed It* reminds me that I am not alone in the world. And as I've gotten older, I've come to appreciate *Barefoot Contessa*, even with the incessant "Jeffreys" and the painfully obvious realization that each episode is a Nora Ephron movie in 26 minutes. Truthfully, it sucks that ain't nobody looking like me anywhere to be found. But here we are.

In my obsession, I've learned that cooking is a form of relaxation for me. An alchemy. A magic I can digest. *Salt*

Fat Acid Heat[2] watches like a hug; I cannot get enough of Chef Samin Nosrat's fascination with what comes from her own hands. I never knew watching Focaccia bread be poked, dented and stretched could be so life-affirming. Recently, I was introduced to Michael Twitty by way of The Sporkful[3] with Dan Pashman. In his episode, he spoke about, among many things, discovering roots you knew were there but along the way got lost. I've discovered that when I don't cook is when I'm out of whack. It's similar to when my room becomes a mess and my chair becomes a wardrobe. When my car is overflowing with sunflower seed shells and my day bag is a detour to Narnia. The signs are there, and my specific correction methods need to be activated. Teach me your ways, Alton. I am yours for the taking.

From my background of fast food and "oh you don't eat pork anymore?", I've picked up the horrible habit of eating my feelings. I don't know when this bad habit got here but I wish the bitch would leave. I can pinpoint its peak: during the chaotic throes of an emotionally, mentally and sexually abusive relationship back in 2012. I've written about it before; no real need to rehash the trash but for the new folks, here goes: he was garbage; a trash human being. He, methodically and with ill intent, made me question every inch of my sanity, worth and abilities. He reveled in finding new ways to gaslight me, telling his

[2] "Salt Fat Acid Heat | Netflix Official Site." 2 Oct. 2018, https://www.netflix.com/title/80198288. Accessed 30 Oct. 2019.
[3] "A Brief History Of American Barbecue - The Sporkful." 10 Dec. 2018, http://www.sporkful.com/a-brief-history-of-american-barbecue/. Accessed 30 Oct. 2019.

friends about my reactions then returning to me with the
news that they thought I was insecure. After he broke up
with me through Google Hangouts and I told him to return
my apartment key, he attempted to win me back and
smooth things over (read: mend his image) when I
realized what had happened to me was abuse. Fun fact:
types like these tend to smell blood in the water. Wade
cautiously and, if need be, punch them in the face. Maybe
not physically, but promise me you'll daydream about it - I
still do. He was discarded but the habit remained.
Eventually, my body began fighting me in protest. The
things I once enjoyed lost all flavor. The act of eating
became a chore. I've since discovered I'm a tactile eater - I
enjoy warming, multi-textured foods. Meanwhile, back at
the ranch dressing, I was shoving full-fat ice cream and the
cheap crunch of Lay's Salt and Vinegar chips down my
throat. My body started to mutiny.

Breakouts.
Irregular cycles.
Constant bloating.
Sore ankles from carrying so much physical and emotional
weight.
Hands cramping and tingling.
Daily headaches.
Loss of range of motion
Drained energy.

I was unrecognizable, even to my own eyes. Something
had to change. After a sudden and dreadful bout with the
flu, the taste for most animal products fell from my

mouth. Chicken, turkey, beef, lamb all lost their luster. The thought of them turned my stomach - not because What the Health had me shook, but because they were and still are reminders of the abuse I'd unconsciously subjected myself to. My being's way of getting my attention was to completely shut down. It pulled me close, sat me in front of me and told me to choose: this habit or my livelihood. That meant consistent releasing of the pain, the "he did this to me!" cycle and acknowledging that this is not a "one and done" process. I'd given away enough of my power during years of a relationship that turned my love and admiration to food into a weapon. I no longer needed him to cut me; I could do it all on my own. The way it played out, I could choose to go or get shot by Harriet. Either way, the slavery to hurt and food had to end. As I write today, I am a practicing Vegetarian that dabbles in Veganism. Practicing as in every day, I practice how to walk out *not* eating my feelings. And sometimes, I fail. I still have my slips and Depression Weight™ has cozied up to me something serious lately. Still, try as I might, I'm that person reading every label on every aisle, the one asking if the salad dressing contains soy, the one you may no longer see at your fave eatery. Every day, I actively choose myself and I take my power back until it naturally finds its home in me.

I can hear the jazz playing, the pans sizzling, the ramekins clanking - on my 4th glass of Thai tea.

Some words on relearning how to eat

#1. Every day is different. I recently completed half of a 30-day body challenge[4] and loved the results. During that challenge, there was no bread, no sugar, no unnecessary food items and eating when hungry. I also was doing 16:8 intermittent fasting so my eating times were strictly regimented. My body was like, "yass sis we love this!". And then my cycle hit. And I lost all motivation. Since that challenge (that I still need to finish), I've been working to find my motivation again with a new caveat: don't be so hard on yourself when tuhday ain't the day. My body has shown me how much she hates sugar, dairy and wheat. It's up to me to listen to her. When I do, my reproductive systems celebrates, gifting me with a less painful and sometimes shorter cycle. When I wild out, I pay for it in pain, bloody pants and belly inches. Sometimes it's worth it, most times it's not. And that's the ticket to any weight plan. Decide if the consequences are worth the mouthfeel. Be patient with yourself, especially your brain. Because your brain is an asshole. Work to push the cravings without denying them. Give yourself treats for work well done. Decide you'll either have the cake or the pizza, not both. Most importantly. monitor your body's reaction to the foods you give it, not just the inches. When you eat dairy do you suddenly cramp up? Does eating bread give

---

[4] "LOSE THE GUTT 30-DAY CHALLENGE - Anowa Adjah." https://anowaadjah.com/shop/30daychallenge/. Accessed 30 Oct. 2019.

~ 38 ~

you brain fog? Your body is telling you some things. Listen and change course.

#2. Recognize your triggers. I'm an emotional eater who craves sugar and salt. Recognizing that has put my eating habits into perspective. It also teaches me the posture of feeling my way through the emotion and not simply denying it. It means mindfulness as to why the triggers are reacting. The worst thing you can do is beat yourself up emotionally then punish yourself physically because you had a human reaction. Be kind to yourself by being proactive. Promise to let yourself feel the next trigger in its totality. Pack yourself a nourishing snack bag to dive into instead of scrounging for something you'll regret later. Scream. Cuss. Cry. Get it out before you let any wayward foods into your body. Giving your triggers room to be aired out assists your process towards a healthy-eating future.

How to hold quotes

"Prayed about it and moved on" - @ohhcami_

"Expect what you accept" - Bari A. Williams' grandmother

"You are not a list of planets or signs. You are the whole damn sky." - Chani Nichols

"It's ok if all you did today was survive" - Unknown

"You betta bash Mister's head in and think on heaven later" - Shawnda Harper quoting The Color Purple

"Connecting to the past and knowing our history makes us both bruised and beautiful" - Beyonce Knowles-Carter

"Blessings can't multiply if you're always wasting energy questioning them" - @astoldbyjayde

"Bitch, say no. It's always more work than you ever wanna do" - Samantha Irby

"I'm not accepting projections today be blessed somewhere else." - @vivrantny

"For every person that has not 'chosen you', know that you have chosen yourself and will continue to do so, always" - @tatiannatarot

"The peace you gain when you realize YOU are your knight in shining armor" - Jada Pinkett-Smith

"If I disappoint someone, it's their loss for putting that expectation on me when they don't know me. I can't control what they want." - Simone Biles

"You want to have the love of your life? Be the love of your life to you." - Asia Sexton

How to start (and maybe not finish) notebooks

Buying new notebooks gives me a rush I can't explain. Deciding which one best suits my mood. Choosing the perfect pen. Does it fit in my day bag? Is this the aesthetic I wish to project? Am I cool enough, and is my notebook saying that even before I part my lips. Don't get me started on ink colors, page thickness and smells.

The closest I've gotten to finishing a notebook is one I grabbed from Walmart. It's a hardcover (fancy) that's small, glossy and bears the words "Ideas & Intentions" on it. I think that's why it's lasted so long - it set its own pace before I even got to it.

My latest says "The World is Waiting". I sought her out with intention, knowing that what she bore would carry more words I have to spill. She fits in my bag perfectly. I consecrated her by writing my dreams in the first page and patting her with money drawing oil. She's green with rose gold trimming, sacred along with the others. This one, however, will be filled and, one day, finished.

Tips on finally finishing a notebook before you start a new one

...

Ok

...

#1. The best one I have which has been working for me is to carry it with you every day, interact with it every day and stay away from the stationary clearance racks.

How Nigga™ is a balm for my weary soul

An excerpt from my piece for The Unmasking[5] in Richmond, VA:

"I was in the 2nd grade the first time I heard the word, 'nigger'. It left the mouth of my favorite teacher, a red-haired, bubbly woman in a predominantly white Christian school in South Richmond, VA. My eyes shot towards her, knowing what I heard was wrong, but no clue as to why. She quickly covered her mouth as the few other Black and brown children all met her with looks of confusion. I think then is where I can mark my realizing I was Black. In 5th grade, I remember a classmate telling us the story of her breakdown in a grocery store aisle, when a man in a Confederate flag sweatshirt told her to move out of his way. In high school, a white classmate and I wanted to date. My dad refused to see that happen using the old, "can they use your comb?" narrative. In 2013, I worked for an outdoor sales company and encountered an episode of both racism and sexism. A client refused to acknowledge me, even as I spoke to him directly. Instead he only spoke to my white, male co-worker. I've been called a nigger on Twitter for my stances, told my natural curly hair isn't "professional". I have been ignored in positions where I had "the nerve to be Black" in that space, spaces nestled in the heart of this city. With this, I began marching,

---

[5] "Program aims to take mask off race relations in Richmond ...." 23 Nov. 2016, https://wtvr.com/2016/11/23/unmasking-race-reality-in-richmond/. Accessed 30 Oct. 2019.

speaking, protesting, opening dialogue and more importantly, listening. In 2nd grade, I first heard the word "nigger." At 29, I've been called that and every other name under the sun. In defiance, for that little girl years ago, in the space I've created, I've added author, creative, entrepreneur, activist and womanist. I choose not to succumb to what they called me."

My ancestors woke up to crosses burning on their lawns. I, a millennial, wake up to unsolicited burning cross gifs in my inbox. My immediate reaction being "my nigga, do you see this shit?"

I have people dear to me who still wretch at the word. There is no love there, no space for us to take back a travesty. To me, we are skilled in it. We are masters at turning tragedy into commodity, sometimes to our detriment. It's for us: we take back that which was aimed to kill us. And draw the weapons down to where they prosper for our benefit.

For me, Nigga in its purest form oils my elbows. It waters my crops. It sees my children off to a productive day at school. Seeing Black men greet each other truly is a sight. The gesturing, the heavy daps, the delight in seeing someone you care for embrace with a resounding "my nigga!". It gives me so much to see how tender it is at its core, even when, on the surface, it's just one of our terms of endearment.

We as a people live out loud in duality - a double, and oftentimes triple consciousness that contradicts and compliments. We tightrope through life trying to find balance in places that are intentionally askew. And for real, what's understood ain't gotta be explained, my nigga.

Some words on how to say "nigga"

#1. Are you Black? If the answer is yes, you can say it or choose not to. It's up to your discretion.

#2. Are you white, NBPOC, white-identifying Latinx? If yes, no tf you can't say it.

Reclamation of a racial slur can only be done by the demographic to which that slur was used. It may not have been birthed from them, but what they plan to do upon reclamation is theirs and not up for outside debate.

#3. That's that on that.

How to shield yourself

You may have never had that person who told you you could do anything. You may have had more people talk you out of instead of into things. You may be one who lives for the obscure and abstract yet they told you the norm was better. Some genuinely thought they were helping; others saw a light in you they wanted and if they couldn't have it, no one could. What about your light draws out the dark? Do you know it's not your fault? Do you know you can protect yourself? Shield yourself, love. It's rough out here for us.

Some notes on shielding yourself

#1 Be sure of who you're shielding. Are you protecting yourself or are you hiding? Is the hiding for growth purposes or because you don't want to face the light? Are you running from the light because it's blinding or because you don't want to be seen? Why don't you want to be seen? Is it fear or shame? Is it both? These are just a handful of questions to ask yourself before you raise your shield. Add to the list until you get to the root.

#2. Hermit Mode is necessary. The Hermit card is the 10th in the Major Arcana. It represents the sign of Virgo, my sun sign. It denotes soul-searching and self-induced solitude when upright, plunging into weariness and withdrawal when reversed. Take the time you need to sort out what's pressing. Similar to the Four of Swords, resting now is required. Cradling yourself in your cave is okay. Full stop.

How to share rituals for your neck, back, pussy and the crack of a psyche

Protect your neck: spend money where it's reciprocated. Line your dollars up in your wallet all facing the same way from smallest denomination to largest. Respeck your funds and they will flourish.

Stop buying your Hoodoo/Rootwork/spellwork/energy things from spaces like Lucky Mojo and white-Hoodoo-derived websites. Shit is fabricated and stolen from Hoodoo and Rootwork traditions. Ain't no such thing as butter candles. Do some research on the suppliers and distributors. If you can't find a face to line up with the name on/of the site, issa fraud.

Protect your back: Get divinations from folk you trust. Divinations are personal prescriptions for the specific situation you're encountering. It's an extremely personal work that come with work - not a flowery gesture or suggestion. Modalities vary: tarot/oracle cards, bones, runes, pendulums, etc. Consult your ancestors to get the real on who deserves your time and treasure. Go with who and what mode speaks to you.

Jar folk who truly deserve it, not just folk who have inconvenienced you. If an ex, family member, co-worker is seeking to do bodily, emotional/mental or financial harm, throw dey ass in a jar. Please note: magic doesn't circumvent common sense. Protect yourself with a weapon, receipts, court orders, etc along with your work.

We stan preparedness on all sides and in all dimensions. The type of jar depends on the transgression(s). Freezer is for those you want to slow down and "chill out". Sour is for those who need to be immersed in the literal shit they're attempting to (or have succeeded) in throwing your way. One of the strongest phrases to speak along with the actions above is "return to sender." Reversal work is nothing to play with. Ain't nothing better than having the spit they flung into the wind hit them square in the face. Protect yourself while doing reversal work so no new attacks can succeed against you. Energy is no respecter of person and it's too easy to get caught in the crossfire. Burn a white fixed candle of protection alongside your reversal work and take those spiritual baths regularly. Now that I think about it... *runs to do bath ritual*

Protect your pussy/bussy/sacred space: no one undeserving of your body should be holding space there, be it an ex, a toxic FWB or that person from the app. Orgasms are actual magic - everybody don't deserve the show. Getting rocks off should come with a price but never at the price of your peace and wellbeing. If you're hung up on that old thing, take a walnut bath (coffee if allergic - safety first) to sever those leftover ties along with conducting a cord-cutting ceremony. As with spiritual baths that involves removing energies, this is a pourover and not an immersive bath. As you heat up your ingredients, speak into the bath the person(s) that need to get up off you AND the strength and self-love to release them. This is a two-way street. We can't want a thing and not do the work in our power along with our folk.

Protect your sanity: While initially studying Hoodoo and getting to know my ancestors, getting overwhelmed came at me fast. I had convinced myself there was only one way to do this work and if I didn't have a specific this or say a specific that, everything I was learning was void. Imposter Syndrome is no respecter of anything. It will show up anywhere, at any time. As we reconnect to lost spaces, shielded spaces, protected spaces, we get lost. We will fight with what is old and secured in our minds and with what is now being introduced. We will be hit with the desire to spiritually bypass the deep work for the sake of saying we've made it. Don't do this. Feel everything. Learn all you can from reputable sources that look like you. Take yourself off the chopping board of belief that says you can only believe one thing at once. Our ancestors spun literal magic from what they knew instinctively, culturally and what they were faced with upon landing on these shores. Break the chains that say it must make sense in order to be real. Your mind will thank you.

Trusted resources:

Daizy October, theafromystic.com

Ifasayo Egunjobi, wildwomendoastheyplease.com

JujuBae, itsjujubae.com

Mambo Elizabeth Ruth, biglizconjure.com

How I write.

I have a scar on my Achilles from 8 years ago. I was in a rush shaving and cut myself down to the literal white meat. The story as to why I was rushing deserves a Drunk History-style telling. Involved was an after-hours club with a friend after receiving the invite from a mysterious white woman who then disappeared into the crowd, the password of Waffles, a babysat glass of Amaretto Sour, Cat Daddies, meeting D-League baseball players, running from my friend's ex, all for me to hurry home at 6 am to pack, shower, cut myself shaving, travel to my hotel room in Virginia Beach to meet a guy who "forgot" to text back. The story slips my mind until I see that scar. Then the vision expands. A wide shot of a day in my life. Often this is how words meant to become stories, poems, essays appear in my life - as one singular thing that takes me down the rabbit hole.

I used to be the poet that needed every line to rhyme to prove that I knew words as a whole ass 8-year-old. I was called to write and recite poems for the school play. The church revival. The family obituary. I sought to speak in a voice worn from experience; to try to speak for everyone in the room. Eventually it wore on me - too young to gauge the emotional intelligence of a gaggle of adults. I even resented the word "poet". Now, as I write, it resembles a fever. The days before you feel it riding up your spine from the bottom on your feet. You know something is taking you over and you wish for when it fully presents itself. Your everything hurts. Laying in bed seeing spots, having dreams and sweating. It finally has laid claim and it's time to fight with it until it leaves your body. Wastebasket full of what needed to be expelled. It tried to kill me, but I wrote my way out. Shoutout to Hamilton. I love you, Lin-Manuel Miranda.

Learning how to write was the first lifesaver the Universe threw to me. Answering the writing call when my spirit cries remains my first band-aid. Healing hurts and my pen acts as the blade, cutting away the dead pieces that are making me sick. I've found healing in pouring out ache that becomes poetry. Writing is my ultimate high, a deep fixation on which there is no clear vision, just the desire to complete what's been started in me. It's how I've survived this long, with prayers from those above acting as semicolons. Healing comes from writing. Words are spells; I teach that to my students, to my child, to those looking to overcome by their written testimonies. It's not the end-all, be-all; it furthers the narratives we speak over ourselves, for better or worse. It can range from a novel to a word. What matters most is getting it out of you onto a page so you can get a good look at it. See what that nagging looks like face-to-face.

Some notes on writing

#1. Do it often. Even if it's just a simple sentence in your favorite notebook. One line on a laptop screen. One word on a sticky note. Do it often to remind yourself of how you sound outside of your brain.

#2. Do it as well as you want to. Yes, there are hard and fast rules. But language also adapts. It grows. It evolves. Change the flow as you see fit. Find the balance between writing that meets the academic marks and the creative ones. Draw the line in the notebook as you determine.

#3. Start over often. Erasers serve a purpose. Backspace has a lane. Etch out how you string together words - stretch the bar as far as it needs to go for you to tell the depth of your story. Rewrite. Toss everything. Keep what's sacred.

How to unravel

There's a thread that runs through this book. A thread that as you pull it, reveals the sides of you you may have run away from or were told to banish. The uncomfortable realities. The eye-widening realizations. That is, our collective unraveling. Yours, the one holding this book and reading this page. And mine, the one writing these words while holding my spools. It's what I've sought to bake into this book in real-time.

My mother was a pro at making me feel like I was never good enough, that I was a mistake, that I was the reason her life turned out the way it did. She will never admit it, mainly because she's unaware of it. It's normal for her to "love" that way. But it's never been normal for me.

I remind my mother of so much. My father never turning up at her doorstep to proclaim his love. The children before she was forced to abort. Me, not bringing her life full-circle. Because I did not live up to the large demands pressed upon me, I was a problem. I imagine in her eyes, I was meant to fix everything. I don't think she much thought about me needing her in return.

She spent a good chunk of my life showing and telling me how much I let her down. I did not know which sides of me offended her, so I set out to shrink all of them. Being reminded of what you've done and even things you managed to do before you cracked the veil can render the most fluid of us immovable. I remember growing dimmer, hoping that my lower light would cause her to not look to me so harshly. Now, I don't know how to fully dream without taking someone else's feelings into account. Every relationship I've had consisted of me shrinking for it to be functional. I couldn't live too loudly, dress too boldly, think too critically or be too open-minded. It's offensive and it means you're ungrateful. Why you would go about seeking to make yourself better when you have everything you need (a house, a job and a *MAN*) proves you only think of yourself. So I shrank even more, not even allowing myself to think a thought before at least three people gave me their approval. I had lost someone I didn't know. The woman I wanted to be was a projection; a safer bet than anything I could dream up myself. How do you save the girl who doesn't need saving? Remove her identity and uplift only the versions of her you'd like to see. The versions you had a hand in creating. She was everything I told others they could be but I didn't believe it. How could I believe in someone I didn't know? I was faking it, hoping I'd somehow make it. Until I picked up Rachel Hollis' book *Girl, Wash Your Face*[6]. No spoilers, but there's a chapter where she speaks on being small. Rather, the demand to make herself smaller. Because living out loud offends people. Because living in any space outside of someone's mental grasp will always injure those dedicated to misunderstanding and miscategorizing

---

[6] *"Girl Wash Your Face." https://www.girlwashyourface.com/. Accessed 30 Oct. 2019.*

you. I saw myself on that page and finally had the wording to unravel myself. That's what that was. That's what I had done. I had shrank myself to near non-existence, all because someone told me to. All because someone saw something in me they couldn't handle and set out to destroy it. In this life, I've dreamed bigger and more vividly. Yet, I still have some trouble deciding what I want on my own. The Universe saw fit to have me go through the hardest stages alone, perhaps because so much of my life had other people's fingertips along the edges. The ancestors sought to give me things I can say I accomplished on my own, so no one could come from the back to claim my rewards - no one could say I made it because of them.

So here we are - threads in hand. We've grown in every way within this one body. We've outgrown in many others. We're offensive, gaudy and powerful with accomplishments on our hips, be it babies and/or businesses. So much of what we have and who we are is by means of what we had the audacity to grow through. Some of our lived experiences we glided through with the grain and others we crawled through with our eyes bloodshot. We now allow ourselves to feel adoration, success and rarified air. Even when it makes us uncomfortable, but especially because the threads we pull apart are repurposed to weave our true existence.

What color is your thread?
How thick is it?
How long does it run?
What have you sown with it?

Some words on unraveling in one piece

#1. Rewiring your brain is necessary. I grew up thinking that whatever I thought about myself was true and was destined to happen. I wasn't wrong - we oftentimes become what we think. But what I thought of myself was complete garbage. I was taught, through word and action, to think of myself as a nuisance. As small. As a mistake. So that's what I became, verbally apologizing for even the smallest of inconveniences. Now, looking back, I see how I created a more toxic environment by believing what I was told. Being right about a negative trait of mine lit up something in my brain that felt like a reward. "See, told you I wasn't shit", was a regular, albeit censored, refrain. Rewiring came when my silent self-talk was heard by people who genuinely cared for me. I couldn't escape their looks of disgust. Not at me, but at the toxicity. I began to see that what I was used to wasn't normal or helpful. It didn't serve as a Jedi mind trick or reverse psychology. It served to lay the foundation of my ultimate demise if I didn't begin rewiring. So, thread by thread, I rewire how I speak to and about myself. It starts by swapping a negative word for a positive, even if it doesn't feel true (yet). If you're at a loss for positive words, ask people who love you for who you are to tell you what they love about you. As uncomfortable as it may be, plant your feet there and listen. Take one or two of their words and add them to your self-language. Say them every day. Put them in your calendar or notes app as a daily reminder to speak them out loud. Again, don't worry if they don't feel true yet. Right now, we're building the habit and clearing the soil. Soon, the seed will take root.

#2. Make peace with the mess. We're in Hermit Mode, right? In the cave, things get messy. Dishes pile up. Laundry languishes. Everything is overwhelming and smells awful. Unraveling while cute doesn't exist. The ugly cries and cold sweats are par for the course. For a less bumpy ride, don't try to fight it. Sitting with the mess doesn't always translate to succumbing to it.

#3. Shadow work is for the bold. Shadow work requires meeting your darkest, most shamed qualities without judgment. Eg: Growing up, adults consistently told me that I was "too much". I was into theatre, on the praise dance team, step team, in the Children & Youth choir, all things where being "too much" is an asset. Instead, it was called a liability. To make amends for my existence (i.e. for the insecurity of others), I shrunk myself. I grew quiet. I stopped dancing, singing, acting. The thing is, that's who I am. My personality, my talents, my essence hit the room before I did and I would stand there in a sea of strangers tamping it down. When you deny yourself the true essence of you, it will keep coming back to the surface until it's acknowledged, sometimes in destructive ways. It took years to realize I was dealing with projection and not an accurate depiction of who I truly am. So, I had to reintroduce myself to the loud me - the one shamed for being herself. Shadow work means releasing the shame.

Shadow work means acknowledging the traits that were deemed "negative" and exploring *why* they were given that label. It means shining a light on the one who has grown in the dark. It doesn't mean excusing behavior, but more so identifying the root and growing from there.

How to be a myth

I met her my freshman year of high school. She was a year older than me in grade and sat near me during Drama class. I was freshly removed from the private school norms I had grown accustomed to and planted frantically into Richmond Public School. It was my choice; the private school options for Black kids in the late 90s-early 2000s were slim pickings. Add to it the socioeconomic pitfalls of distance from school and the higher age range, the chances were increased for racial violence on any given day. I sat in 2ⁿᵈ period while my photo album was being passed around. Even back then I took photos. My bag had at least one of each: a notebook, Green Apple Jolly Rancher suckers and a disposable camera. I took photos of everything and everyone, including classmates. When the book landed on her desk, she thumbed through people she didn't know and stopped when she did. She approached me, holding the blue felt album in her hands. "Why do you have a picture of my granddaddy in your book?"

I had no confidence in these days. I could've been accused of stealing my own work and I would have still found a way to possibly be at fault. My forehead tightened and my voice cracked. An "I...I don't" was all I could muster. "Yes, you do! It's right here. " She tossed my photo album at my hands, his photo landing face-up on my desk. His photo *was* there. He was sitting in between my mom and aunt, the only person smiling. More like a wink. My mother was wearing a boot from a work injury and my aunt stared into the camera in annoyance. This was what I did: take photos and make memories. "That's not your granddaddy, that's my dad," I finally shot back. Her eyes grew big. "What's your name?". At this point, I was still going by my first name. Only family, church and blood, called me by my middle name so I didn't think to offer it. "JacQuetta", I whispered.

"Nah that's not it"

I took another beat before I spoke again.

"...Joi?"

Her eyes grew wider. She moved closer to get another look at the photo, then met my eyes once more. "So *you're* Joi", she told me. I had no answer. Who was I supposed to be?

"You're Joi! I can't believe this!". I sit there confused. Why is this a space for celebration? Was I not Joi this whole time? Was there some gallery of Jois visited only when one fails and you need to boot up another? I was heavy into my Matrix phase so my mind went everywhere. "I've heard about you, just didn't know you really existed! I can't wait to tell everybody!"

Here it begins. Where the landslide of information I was to never find out tore through multiple homes. When hiding in plain sight, it helps to make the mark the person of interest. The person least involved with the plot the center of sight. That was me for years. Some knew I existed; others had a working relationship with me where they knew who I was but I didn't know them. Some bragged on knowing the secret of where I lived, who took me to the pool, who called him out and who enabled. It was a wild ride from sitting at a desk in 9th grade meeting my niece

for the first time to sitting in our living room senior year with my grandmother being introduced to my youngest brother. I called my dad when I learned about my niece. My voice was high - I was beaming. Fourteen years of being an only child culminated to this. "I'm so happy!" I screamed.
"You don't know how much trouble you've gotten me into," he snapped back.

My father was a monument. An activist. A postman. The man you'd see screaming down the mic at city hall meetings. He worked hard to etch out his reputation within the community. Having the physical representation of his indiscretions existing in his space threw a wrench in that wholesome operation. Depending on who was around, I was free to be his daughter. Free to say his name. Free to call him daddy to his face. As I got older, he put distance in between the daddy's girl veneer falling from me with every missed birthday call, every instance of never having holidays together. When he died, I had so much to say. Years of backed-up anger sat in my throat. By him I learned rejection, abandonment, how to make do with the bare minimum, when and why to play small. I learned how to choose partners that wanted all I could give in exchange for nothing. That believing in someone who fails me is my fault. I learned how to hide in the open, how to fake my way through the best intentions and misunderstandings. After my cord cutting, I had finally welcomed the thought that I'd been an orphan this whole time. Neither one of my parents knew how to function in this new reality: one not wanting anything to do with me and the other hoping my being here would change his mind. Two massively broken people collided in ways neither were prepared for. In doing so, they damaged a multitude of people, most deeply their own child.

"Hi auntie!" It's been six years. Six years prior, I met another niece in kickboxing class. Similar scenario: eyes meeting and cutting away in between high kicks and punching wildly. "Joi?". Lordamercy. By now, I strictly answer to my middle name. My first name caused too many pronunciation issues and I just got tired of correcting folk. "Yes?", I said more confidently. "I thought that was you. I'm Brittany. Your dad was my granddaddy". I'm running out of places to put these revelations. She guides me to his gravesite for the first time. I sit there, angry with him and his wife. Feeling disposed of, silenced. I had so much on my heart. My stomach sat in knots but nothing came through. Just the staring of one person into the heart of another and feeling numb. As I prepared to leave, I felt a tug on my leg. A "don't go" left the earth. I stood there refusing to see what he could possibly have to say to me. I heard his voice get caught in his throat. Without looking back, I walked away.

July 6, 2019. I sit at the head of a table in a home belonging to my newest-found niece, a fellow Virgo named Mia. She inboxed me a month prior after finding me on Facebook. "Maybe one day we can meet in real life". From there came details. More revelations. Most importantly, room for my story. She invited me to her home to meet my family closer to my age. As more people came for dinner, I looked around at a table full of people who looked like me. My cousin on my mom's side would always joke that our family is made of mutts, that no one person has a "clear" lineage. There are holes, dark spots, places one ought not go within our family tapestry. I felt a part of the bigger spread but not its more intricate details. Like the string that won't lay flat so it's cut from the final product. At that moment, all eyes were on me.

"She looks like your mama".

"Nah she looks like Auntie!"

"From the nose down, you look like your mama. From the nose up, you look like your daddy".

I sat among nieces, nephews, cousins, all but a handful older than me. I'm asked about what I'd like to know. I'm told about how this side of the family came to be. I'm asked if I'm okay. I'm asked if this is overwhelming. I'm asked if this was worth it. I told my stories, the versions told to me by him so I would stop asking and those of my blood attempting to protect me. He told me I could never see his side of the family because his wife would never allow it. How she caused so many problems for him. Why he could only see me at certain times. Eyes darted around as a collective "nahhhhhh" entered the room. "If she would've known about you, she would've loved you." I say quietly at the table, "I was so worried everyone would shut me down if I spoke ill of him. That my versions of events would offend you all too much. That you'd think I'm making it all up".

"Your story is your story. This was your experience. We don't have the right to tell you what's right and what's wrong. We're happy you're sharing." We talk about his death. We talk about his life. We laugh that Sanaa looks like my great-nephew. I can't help but see how support on this side looks vastly different than what I received.

At times, I'm reminded of how angry I am that I was denied shelter with this side. That I could've had a step-mom, more cousins, siblings. People who may have understood me. I think about what would've happened had I been revealed. Had I not been labeled an urban legend and the feelings of the child were protected over those of the adults. Who would I be? What would I know? Would I had suffered as much, or at least the suffering have a purpose outside of being the scapegoat? I ask this in therapy. She tells me I wouldn't be who I am now if things were different. That their sole mission was to get me here. And for that, there is no better option.

My siblings, living on my father's side, dead on my mother's. For years I knew I was an only child. I still struggle with the fact that I have five siblings each over a decade older than me. I keep in touch with my nieces and nephews. I meet more over Thanksgiving, my older brother giving me the tightest hug. "I'm so happy to meet you."
I ate dinner with them. I introduce them to my child. I come to accept that not all welcome or even understand my presence there and that, honestly, it's okay.

My mind is still blown. This is fodder for Lifetime movies. The moral being: the truth always rises to the top. And answer the DMs.

How to break curses

I became a Reiki II Certified Practitioner in May 2018. I
know my life's work involves healing - myself and others.
My friend told me some years prior that I'd be a healer one
day. I told her I couldn't see it. After some time, her words
began to take root in me and I was reminded of my
fascination with touch as a kid. When my grandmother
would ask me to pass something to her, I would linger
over her hands as she spoke. She'd look at me sideways
and I'd open myself up to the possibility of transferring
energy. Imagine a kid standing, arms outstretched,
focusing with the same energy as Power Rangers before
they morphed. That was me. I would stop breathing,
channel whatever it was really hard and believe whatever
I'm doing is doing something.

I've always sensed energy. From the sudden heaviness to
the whistling of the wind in my left ear to the chill walking
up my spine. It often rings when it's time for me to be
quiet - someone is near and they have something to say.
As I've grown in this gift, I've asked my grandmother to
keep my father away from me. I didn't desire contact with
him. She obliged for a time, allowing him forward only
when he asked me to cut his cord from me. He told me I
had suffered enough under his ill-advised bullshit. I didn't
want to take a meeting with the man who ruined my
mother which caused her to do her best to ruin me. Most
recently, I discovered how so many spaces of love in my
family were wrecked due to heartache and betrayal. The

encounter that changed me was when my last partner broke me. He left me abandoned on the side of the bed to piece myself back together. It finally dawned on me: we had a curse of the unrequited, the left for, the settled-for, the cheated. We women bore the brunt of this curse - calling ourselves loved through a veil of torment. I began to ask what did love mean to me. At the cost of me. I loved to my detriment, spitting out the teeth kicked in by intentional torture disguised as love. I called love a slow pain that would one day be my greatest story. I loved from every drop of my cup *and* the remnants in the saucer. This isn't how love is supposed to work. Learning this lifted such a weight. It also opened the gates to a new way of loving.

I sat with my grandmother and great-grandmother during meditation. I'd been reading the book *Healing Ancestral Karma*[7] by Steven Farmer when I got to the chapter about healing those on the other side. I called out to them. My grandmother grabbed my hands into hers. On this side seeing the color green, I stretched out my hands towards her heart. The ache was still present, even in glory. I felt as it filled with blood, her chest rose as she breathed in enough air to allow herself to cry. Her face broke, tears streaming as she felt it all over again. My eyes began to well. Her pain was familiar. It was sinking, bellowing, loud, crashing. Yet she stood unmoved. Maybe muscle

---

[7] "Healing Ancestral Karma - Amazon.com."
https://www.amazon.com/Healing-Ancestral-Karma-Yourself-Unhealthy/dp/1938289331. Accessed 31 Oct. 2019.

memory. Maybe because this posture felt the most protected. I let us both be vulnerable, the way I wished we could've been when our feet roamed my childhood home together. I told her I love her. My great-grandmother came through orange, her sacral being unloved. She mistrusted herself the same as I do. Because she knew all too well how her words felt being thrown back in her face. How it felt to save people, how it felt to soon after be ignored. Throughout their lives, they were both told they couldn't go beyond others' perceptions of them. That feathers were prettier unruffled. To stand by those who enabled their complacency. It was a safer way to exist. "You have a gift, my love. It is here. Strengthen it. Never let it go", she told me. I open my eyes on the brink of a full collapse. I feel a release I never have before. A curse was broken, a tie severed, a contract torn to pieces. A few more to go. I'm destined - fated - to leave a lasting positive mark on this earth and on my family legacy.

Lying in bed, I reiki myself. I continue to cut my own cords. I discover what got me to this place is generational pain. A tug from deep that feels like pulling a slimy eel from the bottom of my soul. It's still alive, convulsing, wondering why it's been disturbed. Unclogging a well that's sat misused for decades. I wipe my slate clean. I love myself through pain in ways I requested from those who couldn't. I look myself in the mirror and say "I love you" without looking away in embarrassment. It takes effort every day and, truthfully, I don't always succeed. Every damn day I have to remind myself that I matter most to me. It has come at the cost of friends and relationships, yet I lost nothing. No prize was forfeited. My cup is mine. I no longer pour all of me into places with evident holes. And it is not my job to fix them.

Some words on breaking curses

#1. Notice the cycles. What's something that "runs in the family" that's never sat well with you? What's a "tradition" that causes more harm than good? Nine times out of ten, those are the throughlines where curses hide in plain sight. The chaos and trauma have been normalized, and you've been sent here to break the contracts. In doing that, take your time. Some things will hurt to discover.

#2. Do the work. Let me tell you something about running away from your purpose: it always catches up to you, whether we like it or not. I know it's hard. Being the destroyer of curses is a lonely existence. You'll learn how to dodge projections and ridiculous expectations, with most of your work being exactly what you didn't ask for. It's hard being chosen. But you have more control than you think.

#3. Seek out spiritual help. This is where your relationship with your ancestors really comes into focus. You are them, they are you. Go to them with your questions, your fears, your complaints. Reach out to connected elders in your family who are open to speaking on the throughlines. There is how you'll begin to see the curses from the outside, how they manifested in the generations and how (and why) they've been allowed to keep growing. If it's not sound or safe to seek out family help, connect with elders in your community (whichever community that may be).

Many of us build families from friends and social circles. Lean on them.

#4. Be the black sheep. As I said, being the one to take up the banner to break curses is lonely work. You will be vilified, talked about and chastised for attempting to break the familial status quo. The best advice I can give: get cozy and accept the sheep life. You will soon recognize that going with the grain will tear your soul apart. You chose this timeline, this family, this purpose celestially. You know how to navigate this space intrinsically, even if it doesn't appear that way. Trust your gut. And happy breaking.

#5. Break the curses for *you*. In doing this work, we tend to wake up months or even years down the line surprised to see ourselves on the backburner. "I was healing the family," you may say, years of therapy you hoped would trickle down to those who "really need it." But were you? Were you healing *for* the family? Or from them? That act got misconstrued along the way. Because we can't heal for others - we can only heal for ourselves. The act of healing should benefit those we love, just not at the cost of ourselves. Check your reasons why. Ask yourself *why* you've decided to break these curses and if you have the bandwidth/ability/mental & emotional capacity to do so. We can want to heal and save folk all we want. But if we're not strong enough for ourselves, we cannot possibly be strong for others. There's no trap door here; no bypassing of vital self-work to try to save the world. How, beloved?

How can we bypass our wounds to bandage others? Wanting to break cycles simply because it's the right thing to do isn't a good enough reason to start this journey. Go deeper. How are these curses affecting *you*? Start there. Understand that people will fight you along the way. Relatives will be resistant and will flat-out reject your offerings. That will build resentment and you will begin chastising them about work they never asked you to do. As antithetical as it may seem to the greater cause, center yourself here and then, when and if you feel led, begin expanding your reach.

How to righteously gas yourself up

"Ooooooooh bitch. I love myself." I find myself relishing that truth more honestly. I find myself growing more familiar with my skin every day. It's funny being reborn - the shell looks like home but you're so far away from it now. Past a comfort zone - we are submerged in an unlimited wavelength. And we never knew we could reach this far, be this bold, live this loudly. Yet, here we drift. And I ask:

when was the last time you kissed yourself simply for living past yesterday?

When was the last time you took a deep breath?

When did you last cry out your own name?

How have you taken life at different strokes?

When did you last pray for protection even when it was you who brought the smoke?

When did you look to the sky and step out of your own way?

When did you stop living small, quietly, in a constant state of not-good-enough-to-receive-it-all?

When?

Why?

Why not start now? Why not dance in your room, shakin ass and slappin thighs? Why can't I be Beyoncé's Beyoncé to myself? Why can't you be your own masterpiece? Say it now. Say the things that make you cringe but quenches your soul. Say I love you. Say you cute. Say you're unfuckwitable. Because it's all true.

Some words on self-love

#1. Self-love is a journey, not a destination. Rounding the bases of self-love is a dad-to-day activity. Much like healing, you don't one day arrive to never have to work again. It's a near-constant dance of rewiring, demolishing, erecting and affirming. If today is the day you start loving yourself, you have arrived. Celebrate it. You still have breath in your lungs. It's not too late to start the journey.

#2. Learn your language. Yes, we're told to learn our partner's love language to best understand how to love them. But what's your self-love language? What temperature makes your feel most comfortable? Is wearing headphones while shopping peak self-care? What do you love to say about yourself? Does your laugh make you laugh even harder? That's learning your language, the intricate inflections of you.

#3. Get used to receiving. We enter this earth depending on everyone but ourselves. Then one day, us is all we have. How did we possibly miss all the self-nourishing in the middle? Because not only is it not instinctual, it's viewed as selfish. Selfishness harms the collective, therefore self-love is a barred practice for anyone who claims to take care of others. "How can you do both?", society clamors. Why do you have to? Every soul isn't yours to heal. Every fight isn't yours to win. When was the last time you sat down to take in something you love, simply because you wanted to? How many times have you denied yourself the pleasure of your own company? Get used to receiving from you. Whether it's a break or a full breath, rewire yourself to receive because you're here, not solely because of what you have to offer.

How to do rituals

Placing Mahogany Obsidian in my left bra cup, feeling it against my skin throughout the day

Grabbing my boobs in a full embrace anytime I leave my bed, descend a staircase, get bored

Since starting my practice, I've learned that some demons, haints and malevolent spirits laugh at Sage. They sit posted on the walls, inhaling the Sage smoke and growing more insidious like Hexxus from Ferngully. Plus, Sage and Palo Santo are quickly becoming endangered and whitewashed. Imagine getting your spiritual supplies for Sephora. Gross. Please read up on ways to clear your shit without disrespecting Indigenous/First Nations communities.

Camphor has been a godsend. I've burned the resin in an oil burner and added scrapings to a spray bottle for a cleansing room spray. It literally feels like washing the energy of any room. I also burn Bay Leaves, Cinnamon, Eucalyptus leaves, incense. Create a mixture of items most likely already in your kitchen or even your backyard, thank your ancestors and Mother Earth for supplying the herbs and, using a charcoal disk and clay plate, rest your herbs there. Allow the smoke to billow. Carry the plate around your home, being sure to hit corners and under furniture. Use a wood and bristle broom on hardwood floors (a vacuum for carpet). Sweep from the back of your home to the front, gathering energy along the way. Throw out the broom and/or empty your vacuum reservoir as far away from your home as possible. DO NOT dump it in your home. Seal your home with Rose or Florida Water. Place salt at the seals of your home so the bad can't return. Make red brick dust by getting hold of a brick and smashing it to dust. Place at the threshold of your front door. Protect your neck and unstick the bullshit.

Giving more attention to the cards that fly out of my hand during a reading then the ones I was intended on pulling

Also, not feeling so bad for not reading myself often

Praying over my food when it's already in my mouth, asking the spirits to bless the morsels as I enjoy them. Then saying "my bad" for being so fast

Aquamarine yoni egg when I desire some root chakra work

Carrying High John the Conqueror Root at all times in my waking life and paying attention to which palms are itching

Making my Ancestor candles while talking to them like I'm on a cosmic cooking show

Letting myself cry, heaving up the roots of a stagnant reality - something that made me sick, throwing it up until I'm empty

Walking to my favorite tree with an armful of offerings

looking up on a clear night sky and thanking the Universe I get to witness it

Getting strange looks from my neighbors as I perform my moon rituals

Forgetting to write in my New Moon journal then feeling like rules are relative and sometimes arbitrary and writing when and what I feel like

Allowing myself to emerge from the healer closet as many times as I need to

Sitting with my intuition after I ignored it long enough and really, truly listening often while nursing metaphysical bruises/wounds

How to pull in a luminary

I know all too well how to do things for others. How to live for others, how to work for others. What has taken skill is learning how to live for me. My vision of self-love always involves a shower of flowers. Running through a field. Smiling incessantly. In my car today, I realized that the illusion of self-love is far prettier than the actual act, and the act itself can be very simple. How can I change my answers to life's questions? What way can I look at myself differently? Can I accept something I hated before? Can I discover a new way to relate to myself? How can I break down the huge mountain of learning how to love me into small stones worthy of collecting? Worthy of wearing in my bra each day?

I made a sweetening jar for me. I filled it with rose gold glitter, the head of a pink rose, cinnamon, sugar. I speak into it the things that used to make me flinch - the things I now say out loud. I lift me up. I say, "I am loved. I am cherished. I am deserving of every good thing." I tied a ribbon around the neck and I kiss it every morning.

I draw in a true metamorphosis. An event. An evolution.

I look to Solange as she flows into her peak being - an individual who has been reborn over and over again, each evolution bringing her closer to her highest form.

In my brain, I'm trying to get to Z while sidestepping some letters. I know I can't do that. Still, I'm hoping Mother God blinks this one time and lets me pass through unscathed. I have days when I want to go to sleep for 6 months then wake up with all the answers. Another impossibility.

"Who do you do this for?". I ask myself.

"The me I haven't met yet."

My thoughts are, when I learn to love me right, she will appear. Because it's home. It's the space in which she's most familiar.

Some words on creating space in the cocoon

#1. Stretch your legs. Getting used to kicking against a thing until it breaks. It's how you get free.

#2. Learn to breathe underwater. At one point, the caterpillar is immersed in what it's becoming. This substance is designed to choke out what no longer belongs, strengthen the lungs and the caterpillar's capacity to handle change. It's a viscous enzyme, eating the caterpillar alive. After it is swallowed up, pretty sure it's gone for good, it emerges anew. It quickly adapts to its new surroundings. The adversity once thought to destroy has fortified this new being. Allowing what is currently going on around you to build you into who you're meant to be will help you redefine the adversity versus succumb to it.

#3. Find something new. A new way to move that defeats the old. A new way to wait when the doors are sealed and the windows stuck. Soon, the wings will have no choice but to spread.

#4, Give in to the dark. There is no light without darkness. And darkness will attempt to swallow you as you vibrate higher. My tip is: give yourself over to it. Not to succumb, but to grow. We've talked about Shadow Work: the act of getting to know intimately the sides of you birthed in shame. Find out why you act the way you do, why certain innocuous things are triggering, how and why shame has played such an integral role in your life. Receive that information. Accepting that person - the one you were told is useless - instead of continuing to hide them goes the farthest in your healing work.

How to breathe fire

I've doused the flames inside me

afraid to light new ways of existing

to kick up dust

instead I've swallowed embers and burned myself

because I've been doing this all wrong

the key to breathing flames is to

inhale them deep into your esophagus

ease down the lining of your throat

down to the top of your diaphragm

where it licks at what you truly feel

truly mean

at the heart of your rage you keep tamping down

instead of learning how to properly inhale

the smoke is choking you for a reason

It's demanding you learn how to breathe

call a mountain down to its knees

command trouble to be cast away

never to lick near you again

we're exerting too much energy

fighting what we have already conquered

with just a word

it's demanding you spit fire and flame

so you can live and not die

How to not "turn out fine"

My mother once bragged that when she dies, everything she owns will belong to me. A tortured soul, this was her way of bonding. She reveled in her abilities to pay me in things I never wanted - her love language being gifts and announcing I wouldn't have anything or be anyone without her. As a result, I'm just now living my life as I desire and not how she sees fit. Maybe because she felt stuck where she was - in a home never built for her.

In 2014, I began the process of taking over ownership of my childhood home. Joyce had become emotionally mute, refusing to deal with the work that came with owning that home and the fight over what was left. I had so many ideas: it would become a home again for a needy family, I would sell it and create a memorial fund in honor of the ancestors we'd lost. The last-case scenario would be I fix it up and live in it myself. I refused that last option; it was too familiar, too much representing a cycle I was done repeating. So I reached out to family, told them my ideas and expressed that I was open to theirs. Three cousins responded. No work was done. I got back mutters and the judgmental "well..." with an inflection I've come to hate. Many blamed my mom's alcoholism as to why the house fell to pieces. These same people never helped toward the cause of either - the house or my mom. So I began again for a third time. The house had been broken into, ransacked, family heirlooms stolen, made a home for the transient. We went in with literal guns blazing and took in the damage.

Old bookbags used as pillows.

Family photos broken in their frames.

Glass everywhere.

Every electronic gone.

Awards ripped in half.

Bible cassette tapes still intact.

I wanted to cry from sadness. I wanted to explode with anger. I was angry she let it get this bad. Angry no one else bothered to help. I gathered all that was worth taking and made my exit. There was nothing to save here. By all accounts, it was dead on our arrival.

As explained to me, Joyce acquired the house from my great-grandmother, her dad's mother. We moved in when I was three. There was a cinder block etched with the year 1991 on it. From jump, I had no place to truly call my own. Not my own room and barely anyone to talk to. I lived with both my grandparents as well as my mother. We were all argumentative; being passive was a slap in the face and viewed as weakness. Here is where I honed my grit, my sarcasm, my love for irreverent comedy and how to time out a response. I never had sleepovers outside of family - there was nowhere to put them and, even if there was, no one in that house had patience to deal with me on top of outsider-ass versions of me. There were days I hated coming home. I felt so isolated and war-ridden. The highlights were family gatherings where I could be my most extra and folk would simply laugh and say I'm showing off. I was a nerd. Still am a nerd. A bookworm, I fell into the wormhole of Harriet the Spy and Babysitter Club books. I never snuck out. Never had wild parties. Joyce grounded me once which we both knew was laughable (how do you ground someone who barely goes anywhere?). I made holes where I could, spaces in the house where I carved some place of belonging. A nest made of clothes, my grandmother's room after she moved downstairs. I treaded lightly and as loudly as I could. I wanted to be seen, more so acknowledged.

In Spring 2017, years after my grandparents died, I drove down the street where I learned that we don't walk on sidewalks and "we" don't go to "that" pool. Where I was raised on HBO and MTV. The bones had been exposed: the house was being torn down. If you've ever played on a construction site as a kid, you're familiar with that eerie feeling of organized destruction. There's a mixture of calm and chaos. Life and death by way of bulldozers. You feel like you're part of the wrecking crew, like you have the ability to tear down everything. Walking up to what was left, something strange happened. I felt the house give up the ghost. Better yet, I felt my grandmother give up hers. She was finally free to go after being stuck for so long.

Emotionally - spiritually - mentally, home for me is different from a house. Home is where you not only lay your head but also your worries. Where you begin again, eat, sleep, make love. A house is worn bones picked over after home dies, if it ever lived.

I had a vision of walking through the skeleton on which my last home stood. Dreaming someone else's dream. Maybe even the dream my mother had. There aren't many good memories to hold on to outside of holidays. I more remember ache. Sorrow. Anger. Regret. It was stuck in the walls and no amount of varnish could pull it to the surface to be cleaned. I stood there at the feet of the ruins. All those things, powers, sorrows - gone. At least from this place.

I always had cousins that asked how I managed to live in the house alone, a kid, just me, with Nonee, Big Daddy and Joyce. Now that I think about it, I truly don't know. As my grandmother got sicker, she became more loving. Maybe it's the guard we women of this family put up. Afraid to get hurt and afraid to acknowledge the hurt we've caused. A cousin once said to me, "We come from a family of proud, opinionated women who don't know what the hell they're talking about." My perspective changed soon after. Finally someone said what my mouth couldn't but my heart had always known. Perhaps it's work worth doing. Perhaps I'm the one who grew up in it and decided not to fan the flames any longer - instead to walk away. And I'm here hailing from ashes called home.

Some words on walking away.

#1. Do it for the sake of your peace. My mother peered over her glasses as we sat in family therapy for my daughter and proclaimed to mostly herself that I "turned out fine". My daughter's therapist sat up in her chair awaiting my response. My eyes darted around the room, resting on the face of each person present before raising my own declaration. "I've been in therapy for nearly 13 years. Since freshman year of college I've sought professional help. I did not turn out fine". Your peace matters most. Anything that comes at the sake of your peace is too expensive.

#2. Do it fast. What tends to hem us up in needing to walk away is the slowness in which we do it. We think, even hope, that something will happen in the time it takes to finally leave that will change the heart of the person we're walking away from, and we want to be there to witness it. Nine times out of ten, that will never happen. That person isn't going to miraculously change course because they're afraid of losing their place in your life. If anything, it justs hold you closer to the fire from which you need to escape. Don't second guess. Get away while the thought is fresh and you have the ability to go.

#3. Do it often. When love is no longer being served, get up from the table, flip that bitch and go build your own. Do this as often as you need to. If you're someone like me who was raised to doubt your voice and needs, leaving a situation can bring up guilt. The guilt will cause you to stall out as you've most likely been taught to center the feelings of others and not your own. Learn to love how your feet hit the ground as you walk away. From rejection, projection, lack of accountability and disrespect. The more often you do it, the more familiar your body will become to owning your power and autonomy.

How I began reclaiming my time + body

TW: partner assault/oral rape

Sometimes the mind breaks down on you. You forget details. You pass something off as just a thing that happened. Like the time an ex-boyfriend intentionally slammed my open mouth onto his penis during oral sex. I had asked him not to hold down my head as it hurts when he did. He agreed. I trusted his word. He did it again, this time holding me down harder while attempting to bounce my head and not let me move. I couldn't breathe. I jumped back and screamed. I trusted him. He blamed me, his obsession with a certain porn act and past girlfriends who let him do it before. It was punishment for "ruining the mood" and not getting into his "kink". I was driving to work over five years later when it all came rushing back to me.

I didn't know what to do with this information. The remembrances of the condom being removed in the beginnings of my last relationship. When I asked him if he removed the condom, he told me things "looked clean and he wanted to see how it felt". Me pulling away and him attempting to coerse me back into sex, which I refused. The senior during my freshman year in high school cornering me after confessing he liked me and told me to touch his penis. The unwelcomed dick pics. The demands to smile. The threats that I'd better minimize myself or be forever alone. I took all of this to mean I was broken, an attraction only to worse broken men who deemed me acceptable. I took this to mean that my lot was to wade through garbage while pussy-poppin for my man at the time. Religion told me my body wasn't my own. Society agreed, adding anything that happened to it was of my own doing. Two convoluted thoughts existing in one space. A breakdown at 12 years old during winter break triggered some repressed memories. I can't tell you how or why. I began to speak about my molestation from ages 8-10. I struggled with the parts where I liked the attention my molester was giving me. It was the only time someone paid me any mind. I left out that I thought it was normal; that this was just a part of growing up. That no one explained that this was wrong so it must be okay, right?

I sit and think about this from time to time. What would've happened had someone intervened. If someone told me it wasn't right, safe or regular. Where would I be? What would I have done? Would I not have attacked and shunned my own body in penance? Would I still had waited until marriage to have sex because I was so ashamed? Would I still regard my body as a burial ground for abuse?

It's taken me years to learn how to love every inch of me. I'm still reconciling being a sexual being with the events that have taken place over the course of my 32 years. It almost feels audacious. Brazen. Like going from one extreme to the other. Within growth, within unashamed trips to the adult toy section, within owning my version of sensuality, I've found a voice airing out harassment and calling out aint-shit, toxic behavior. It has not been easy here. There are the dark days where I attack myself, ask myself why wasn't I stronger, why did my brain forget these details? I remember the traumas. The attempts to move forward and put them past me. The fear and loathing of my own body.

I sat with myself one day as the guilty feelings were attempting to push through. I asked, "what's the truth here? Why are you feeling this way?". This is where I truly started to unpack and this gem was revealed: "You did not fail. You were failed. Every adult that should've protected you, failed. This isn't on you".

Let that sink in as I continue to do the same.

There are days my walk is nothing less than legendary. Days I take double glances in a passing window and twerk for no reason. Days I touch my body in ways no other can. And there are days I can do none of those things. Both are valid.

Some words on reclaiming your body after sexual trauma:

#1. I'm still learning. Since starting this book, I've been working to obtain my Sexology certification. Because my way of understanding something is to dive headfirst into it, what better way to explore the thing that caused so much shame in all its glory? My focus is on sexual reclamation after sexual trauma, be it molestation, sexual assault, rape, sexual violence, body shaming and religious dogma. Fully reclaiming my body is an exercise of grit and humility. It's full time work with bumps and bruises and fears and missteps. But it's something that I can't see myself not doing now. One tool I've picked up and have used on myself is an exercise explained in *Pussy Prayers*[8] by Black Girl Bliss. When you're mentally and emotionally open, start by placing your hand on the part of you that was traumatized. This may take some building up towards as we tend to shame the body part more than the perpetrator. Hold it and for now just say "I see you", "I feel you". Give no shame, accept no shame. Take as much time as you need here - don't allow any thoughts to rush you. Sit, cry, lament, wail, scream. Do whatever invites the purest intentions. And build from here with your own rituals. There is no wrong way when it comes to your

---

[8] *"Book Store — Black Girl Bliss | Sacred + Sensual Self-Care for ...."* https://www.blackgirlbliss.com/book-store. *Accessed 30 Oct. 2019.*

reclamation, as long as you're safe, giving and asking consent and living your truth.

How to get your nipples pierced

Do I love myself enough to endure pain the likes of initial breastfeeding? For the chance to say I did it? Because they look so cool? And I love being the one looking at them?

Yup.

The date was September 4th, 2015. Beyonce's birthday. Two days after my own. I sat at my work desk pretending I really love this job in a bit of a conundrum. Should I or shouldn't I? Why and why not? I'd been playing with the idea (and fake piercings) for some months now. I had people volunteer to sit with me while I turned over my boobs to the huge yet gentle hands of the bald piercing guy. I went to the piercing shop once on recon and left queasy. It took me years to get my first tattoo - 4 to get my second. I take this shit seriously.

That day at my desk I slapped myself figuratively. "What you gon do? What do you have to lose?". I left work and drove down to Lucky 13 by myself, telling no one I was about to become a Tumblr vixen. We loved a Tumblr Vixen. To me, she is the woman bare naked basking in the slotted rays of sun on the floor reading Octavia Butler. She has a gigantic fro and her skin is the texture of watercolor paint. She is perfectly imperfect, of every size, shape and shade. She is unashamed, loud and uninhibited. I wanted that in my own way. Also, RIP Tumblr and female-presenting nipples.

I walked in wearing a scowl. I was not here to play myself. I'm walking out of here with piercings, dammit. I changed from my regular bra to a sports bra. I read that's what you're supposed to do. I research EVERYTHING. My face is still in game mode: cheaters never prosper, protect this house, ANYTHING IS POSSIBLEEEEEE! The piercer I met on my initial recon mission greets me warmly and tells me what to expect. I sit there stone-faced, not letting any sense of fear cross my disposition. He pulls out two gauges which take me off-guard. "Whoa. I...I thought these were done by gun?", I stammer. "Oh no, these particular piercings are done manually." My face cracks. The mask is lifted. My stomach drops out of my scared ass.

Me: "sooooooo I uhhh... ok. Give me a minute."

He sits back and pretends not to be slightly annoyed by my falling apart. I'm fidgeting. I'm sweating. I'm wall sliding due to said sweat. He comes to me after me jerking from him at least three times and reminds me how it felt to breastfeed x 10. Afterwards, I fell to the padded table, woozy from adrenaline and laid there until the room stopped spinning. I tried to listen to music but it just mocked me. I tucked my new bad-ass boobs into my now too-tight sports bra and tried to remember how to walk without bouncing.

Since my initial piercing session, I've gone back to have them repierced. One closed within five hours of changing my jewelry. FIVE HOURS. It took me a year to build up the courage to sit (let's face it, lay) in the booth again. The second time was with a woman and went much faster. Barely a pitch. So there's that. I've since gotten a nose ring and am now entertaining getting my third tattoo. I'm leaning towards a colorful illustration of the Nine of Pentacles. Because Virgo and badass blitchery.

I was recently asked why go through the trouble for something only a few would see? I answered because I can. On my radical self love journey, I've become more of an exhibitionist. More people have seen and complimented my pierced nipples in group chats and after-dark forums than lovers. And I'm loving it. Having something as a secret I can choose to share is powerful to me. It gives me a boost when the unexpected is revealed and appreciated. I hug my boobs tight every day; when I'm descending a staircase, running to the bathroom in the middle of the night, when giving myself hands-free orgasms. They are a work of pierced art, dammit. That's why.

Some words on adjunct badassery

#1. Do the thing that scares you. I can't imagine my brown biddies not being pierced now. But I was, for a while, worried about other peoples' perceptions in case they ever found out. Now, I go braless when I feel like because so the fuck what. It's no secret my nipples poke through sheer dresses. The bar or hoop outline is there. I'm not ashamed and I actually get a lady boner from thinking about who can see them. And that's fun. Do the cool/scary/badass thing because you can. You'll get such a self gas-up because of it.

How to mother a dope kid

Look, motherhood can be miserable.

In 2019, I have a ten-year-old daughter. She's named after my grandmother and she came to me when I wasn't ready for her. I cried for three months, convinced my body was deceiving me. I had a horrible pregnancy and a delivery that culminated in an emergency c-section, a failed epidural, two blood transfusions and a scar across my soul. I was beyond wounded; I was shattered. For years I wasn't close to my child due to what I now know was Postpartum Depression. I had no idea that trauma during childbirth could trigger such evasive tendencies. I blamed her, I blamed my circumstances, I blamed God, I blamed myself. I've navigated a divorce, single motherhood, failed relationships and the abolishment of family curses with her by my side - but I didn't treat her well. And one day, after coming home with a bad grade due to testing anxiety, more so due to me demanding perfection, I witnessed her brokenness up close. I saw her cracked open and afraid, looking for someone to hold and finally see her. Instead of averting my eyes, I let myself see her. And I apologized. For all I could remember. For all she has ever known as her reality. For the missed hugs and short patience. For my projected anger and fear. For failing her up to this point. And told her it's her choice whether she forgives me. That was the first time I let my daughter see me. Not the author. Not the mom. But me - as a torn-open shell of a woman. After that, we've flowed. I'm learning how to mom in real time - how to mother both her and myself. We started therapy when she was eight. I owned up to my bullshit - some honestly believed, most chewed on as passed-down rationalities. I still yell. I still lose my patience. But through a constant gut check and my words spoken back to me through her, I hold her for no reason. I kiss her in front of her friends and she beams. I gas her up just because. I dance with her and watch her soar because that's what she's here to do.

She wore her hair in locs from ages 4-8. Because money was tight and kids can be assholes, she was bullied. So much so that she attacked her scalp with scissors, cutting many of her locs down to the roots. I was angry. Horrified. Worried that cutting her hair could lead to cutting in other ways. She was the only little girl whose hair was loc'd. They fell on her face so beautifully. As she got older and they grew longer after reattachment, they became a part of her signature. One day, she cried she wanted her hair to be like mine. I tried to convince her to reconsider. We have different hair textures, mine being more 3b-3c and her's being a rich and thick 4c. I explained she wouldn't have the same look as me. I worried more about bullying. I pleaded with her to change her mind. Then I realized I was making her choice to rewrite her signature about me. I was acting like those I wrote about in earlier - more concerned with what outsiders would think instead of her need, even if I didn't agree. We made an appointment to do the big chop. I still have her locs in hopes that one day they'll be reattached. But I know that's my dream and it may never be hers. I'm moving towards being okay with that.

One day, I hope she reads this with the honesty in which I wrote it. Through the fire, she became one of the brightest, most kind pillars of strength I know. She's seen a hell some adults can't fathom. She smells of candy and smoked cinnamon, nail polish and watercolor paint. Sanaa is tiny Angela Davis, with a fight honoring those who came before her while she blazes her own path. She's not infallible; she's tender and hasn't fully learned how to love herself. How many of us do? We relearn that posture if we ever learn it at all. I've learned to love me through her.

On any given day, I marvel at this really cool thing she's done. Whether it's finding her voice, loving herself now, deciding enough is enough. For her, it's just Wednesday.

My word for mothering a dope child while mothering yourself, taken from an excerpt I contributed to the site Raising Mothers[9]:

"Parenthood is the mountain. A mass of matter with seemingly insurmountable peaks and cold, deathly valleys. I question still, 10 years later, why I chose this trek. The body dysmorphia and muscles still numb to the touch from c-section scars oftentimes match my numbing depression. I try to find pockets of happiness in waves of regret. I don't regret my daughter; I regret bringing her into this family with these ails and all this shame. She comes from pain; a fiery preteen mad at everything and everyone while I, her mother/greatest cheerleader/harshest critic, works to mother her and myself in real-time. Parenthood is a wildfire. And in my prayers, I bake in the hope she and I will rise triumphantly from our respective ashes."

---

[9] "Parenthood is the mountain: 13 mothers define parenthood ...." http://www.raisingmothers.com/parenthood-is-the-mountain-13-mothers-define-parenthood/. Accessed 30 Oct. 2019.

How to return from your return

29/30/31 - Saturn Return[10]

(Written August 2018)

When you realize you missed out on most of your life, that your voice has been muted as you screamed from the top of your lungs, you've swallowed blood and called it nourishment, you time out and set out to live as loudly as possible. I've been learning this on the cusp of my 31st birthday. The year 30 has pulled from me lessons I thought I'd already aced. I have cornered heartache, betrayal, psychosis, nights with a dry throat and crusty eyes. I've seen myself, been active in my mind and body for the first time in probably ever. I listened to myself and didn't flinch. I am actively opting out of running down the list of the wrongs done against me and the wars I've waged against myself. Continuing to cry over well-saturated soil guarantees nothing will take root. Instead, I turn my focus to the seeds I carry with me and drop along the way. I'm a subject matter expert in me. I still need reminders to love myself outloud and in the quiet. To set and keep my boundaries. To be my truest, left-of-center, cosmic-embodying self. My life, the next 100 years, my descendants depend on it. So I'm here, with a new understanding of a sacred process. It has no set course;

[10] "Your Saturn Return: A Cosmic Rite of Passage - Astrostyle." https://astrostyle.com/saturn-return/. Accessed 30 Oct. 2019.

your first step acts as the initiation to who you're deciding to become.

Some words on navigating your Saturn Return

#1. Be prepared to go back to move forward.

Now at 32 and officially on the other side of my return, I can share that all manner of shake-ups occur during the meat of this journey. Relationships end, friendships splinter and who you knew yourself to be is completely upended. My best advice? Ride the wave as steadily as you can. There's no wrong way but intentional regression. Regression is a real thing during growth, and because healing isn't linear, taking a few steps back is often required. The key is to learn from and pass the lesson being reintroduced by regression. No sense in beating yourself up - this is the time to remember and acknowledge the red flags you've ignored, the yeses that masqueraded as nos and really act on your newly-gained wisdom.

#2. Pay attention to cycles and patterns.

I cannot stress this enough. Pay attention to repeat cycles and patterns. What looks like just a repeat lesson is the Universe giving you the chance to correct past mistakes and acknowledge blind spots. It's easy to rebuff these, especially if you've made major progress. Instead of doing that, always ask yourself, "what am I missing? What's the lesson here?" This helps to release that pressure course correction applies (and let's be honest, we add to that pressure by way of misplaced perfectionism). Don't fall for the okie doke. Acknowledge the repeat patterns and adjust how you move.

Breathfire deux

I had a curse that was the gatekeeper of my life
It came through hungry
Sent by an ancestor to afflict my mother
My lineage
Me
It clogged up the pipes
Allowed dribbles to pass
Told me to be thankful for bare bones

I stood in my kitchen when it poked at me
"Face me"
We lock eyes
Stop fucking with me
Stop fucking with my life
My money
My love life
My past lives
The lives I have left to live

My child
My future partner
My mind, oh my mind

Leave me forever the fuck alone

I send back your curse
Your broken mirror shards and shattered glass
Your penchant for cutting open healing wounds

Your directions for living the very worst life
And I reverse it back to you
Even on the other side

You no longer lay claim here
I am saving me
God in me
My higher self
I am protected
By a light you can never penetrate
Those protecting me behind the veil are behind you
making sure you pay for your sins against me

How I conduct my readings

How I intend:
fresh awakening every morning with this as routine as
breathing
all crystals charged, all hearts and minds clear
Ancestors are called down to join in on the mood
A clean slate
Multiple shuffles
Clear definition of why I'm here
Rosewater in air

How it actually goes:
after 3 days of wondering why I feel so disconnected,
I remember my deck is in my bag
I hesitate and try really hard to clear my mind
I remember trying that hard doesn't work for me
I listen to my ancestors
I shuffle until I know it's time to pull
I take a breath
I get ready to receive

How to say "fuck this shit"

The hardest day of my life was waking up the morning after my 31st birthday and wanting to die. I had no plan; no real desire to hurt myself. I just wanted the agony to stop. The next morning, I heard a sinister voice whisper, "you should just die."

I at one time had a deep martyrdom ideation. Because the greatest way to show love is to lay down your life, right? I wanted so badly to be loved that I died emotionally, spiritually, mentally. I confessed to my therapist what my brain was doing and it was the first time I let tears form behind those words. I was so unsure of how I got to that point or where to go next. I preached self-care and here I was, depleted. I modeled Black Girl Magic without a spell to my name. Not a prayer. Just a wish to no longer be here. "Did you have a plan?", my therapist asked me. "No." I whispered. "You know, many people who have contemplated or even attempted suicide and lived to recall they didn't want to die; they just wanted the pain to go away."

And that was it - I so desperately wanted the pain to go away.

Since that moment the phrase, "the importance of living" has stuck with me. What does it mean to live? We most see it depicted as doing the thing that causes the most fear, like jumping from an airplane or presenting that scary speech. But what if the scary thing *is* to live? What if the offensive, threatening thing *is* to keep going? How do you do that?

What I've discovered is that there is no set way. Beyond the veil, beyond the manufactured weaponry aimed to fire when we come to this realization, is the deep recognition that living by and for anyone else is complete fucking bullshit. And we decide to live for ourselves. It may offend our mothers whose wounds we told ourselves are ours to mend. It may threaten our circles who said they'd be there no matter what. It may mark you an outcast and cause you to step out of line. You may be shunned. You may be ridiculed. You will lose friends and relationships along the way. But you will find you. The wrinkled, singed, tucked away you who now finally has the chance to live in full. Choose that, and fuck the other shit.

Some words on saying "fuck that shit"
#1. Happiness Isn't Good Enough.
Plead joy. Require joy. Because happiness, especially
given from outside sources, will always be fleeting. Find
what brings you joy even in the smallest doses. Up your
doses as you see fit. Start from within.

#2. Find a dope, understanding therapist.
If you take little else from this book, take the advice of
finding the best therapist for you. Identifying and working
through my martyrdom ideation has also helped with
suicidal ideation and negative thoughts. I understand the
fear of sitting on a "couch" and pouring yourself out to a
complete stranger. It's daunting. But please, take the
leap. You will be so much better for it.

#3. Sometimes all you can do is exist. Be a mound of
matter taking up space. Even there, you are valid. You are
designed to take up space despite what the awful people
and thoughts have told you. Continue doing so. Because if
you haven't been told, I'm glad you're here.

How to be both Black and a woman

Double-minded with echoes of intuition. "Who are you supposed to be beyond the hurt?" I touch my face. I pen myself four letters. One to my heart, one to who I was supposed to be, one to who I am, one for forgiveness. It's summer and my window is open. The air is thick with intention and surrender. In one night, I went from muted saturation to technicolor. Sunflower seeds dot the night sky cracked between my fingers. We cute in this space, smelling of amber, wearing the nerve to exist unapologetically.

I've gotten into many a comment war with men, specifically Black men, calling my plight as a Black woman into question. The composite of Peak Black Woman in the wild: thin waisted with phat ass, thighs and hips, buxom and birthing the world through sheer will and power, bronze with head held high, impervious to every single negative word sent her way. This is the echelon, and anything less than is a slight to the entire community.

I spoke on a podcast that we don't get the space to be both Black and a woman. We are often expected to choose. The men in the room let out a chorus of "hmms." I continued that being both in any given space causes discomfort, a level for which I will not apologize. I embody a duality of existence. I'm no monolith. I don't have to tear myself down to give you an ego boost. I am unabashedly a

Black woman. I will not divide myself across the blade to cape for one side and deny the other.

We are the first to be abused. The first to be ridiculed. The first to be rejected. Yet, we are those the masses beg to kiss their scars and their asses. Our men silence us, saying what happens here stays here, reminding us that their mothers/grandmothers/aunties endured this pain, so why can't we? The fact that we aren't built like the generations before us is viewed a liability when in truth it's an undeniable asset is soul-crushing. No, we aren't built for agonizing emotional labor, abuse in plain-clothed love, sitting back and allowing our destruction because being Black matters more than our personhood. We aren't built for romanticized, church-sanctioned abuse doctored up to look like loyalty[11].

You would think Black men would look at what lies in front of them and call it what it is. That Grandma never left because every institution was designed for her to stay. That the marks across their aunt's body weren't caused because she liked to talk back. That your mother wasn't "too strong", but too audacious in believing in herself for others' liking. You would think a Black man would look at that and go, "Nah, this is some bullshit." You'd hope that

---

[11] "Who Protects Us from Our Protectors? - Joi Donaldson - Medium." 3 May. 2017, https://medium.com/@joi_unspeakable/who-will-protect-us-from-our-protectors-68685ffb9f1. Accessed 30 Oct. 2019.

they would rise up against such a disgusting will. Yet, too many rest in groupthink and nothing changes - too afraid to stand up against the very system of traditional thinking that binds us all yet benefits a few.

The rest of the world turns a closed ear. We are conditioned to believe that love must be birthed from torture and pain, then we still have to wait until someone deems us worthy. Fuck that. I'm worthy where I stand. You're worthy where you stand. I fight for every Black woman. My trans sisters, my marginalized sisters, my broken sisters, my loud sisters. Even my sisters who would see me dragged and called every name in the book because I don't center my Blackness to deny everything else. I am both Black and a woman. And I stand for the healthy and correct treatment of every part of me.

Some words on being a Black woman
#1. There is no greater superpower. There is no greater heartbreak. In being in this skin, in this body, presenting as I do, I know despair all too well. I also know the triumph I've earned with every lash against my skin. In whatever capacity you stand - as a cishet Black woman, a Black femme, Black non-binary femme presenting, Black trans woman - I see you. I honor you. Let's keep giving these folks hell.

How to greet Tuesdays

I don't know what I did to piss off Tuesdays. Maybe because they heard me whisper I prefer Thursdays. Maybe because it's considered Monday Jr. or Wednesday Lite. Maybe due to its incessant need to be cooler than the rest of the days. It will never be an early Saturday morning on an autumn day and it knows it. So maybe that's why they hate me. But I'm grateful to see them every time they roll around.

Some words on Tuesdays

#1. They will never been Thursdays.

#2. Be grateful for them anyway.

How to feel seen

I sat on the couch of a woman who decorates her office to make it feel like a home outside your own. She has locs dipped in watercolors. She has a favorite lamp that went missing once before our session and I watched her get mad as a coworker "returned" it. I've watched her laugh and tear up with and for me. At our first meeting, after I emptied out my chest to her, then a stranger, she looked me in my eyes and said, "I see you". I met her after a fellow clinician reached out after my social media cry for help. "I need new coping skills," I said behind red eyes, devoid of resolution and hope. "Give me your information. I want to send you to my colleague."

I had put into the universe that I desired a Black woman therapist. My previous therapist, who was a white woman, understood the struggle of being the child of an alcoholic, but didn't give me what I needed in regards to being a Black woman navigating existence in America, let alone Trump's America. Being given what I needed in a time I was fully falling apart really showed me I'm not just yelling prayers at the sky. They actually do get answered.

I sat in her office with a box full of my limbs, toxic religious ideologies, my martyrdom ideation, PTSD, suicidal thoughts and bags that didn't belong to me but I carried anyway. Growing up in church, we're taught to take on others' burdens, confessions and dark secrets, never being told of the consequences. The heaviness and silence of

Depression & Anxiety were my daily norm. I began to unpack. Until that moment, unpacking always came with a caveat: I could only unpack to a degree, to a level that was deemed comfortable for the receiver. Anything outside of that was mine to deal with. She watched me flip over my box. First, she gave me a safety plan and instructed me to list what I normally do in a spiral and a healthy alternative. I struggled to finish it. I told her I felt guilty that my child wasn't the first person I thought of when it came to saving my life. "Ma'am, who told you your daughter had to be the first person?", she warmly chastised. "Because I wanted to have that type of bond with her. But I know it's suffocating. That doesn't belong to her, to worry about me, to feel like I do anything for or because of her. That's not fair in my eyes. But I'm not sure of how to express that properly." Guilt is more familiar to me than understanding. She looked at me: "This is *your* safety plan, and whatever you decide to put here is for you and only you. There is no guilt here. Who told you to feel bad about that? That that made you a bad mother?". I didn't have an answer. I never knew that could be an answer. I again took the familiar way out and blamed myself. She lovingly stops me when I haven't taken a breath in a while. I have roots hanging from my lips from seeds I was forced to swallow. I have been raised to not trust myself. Parts of my background aren't uncommon yet so is seeking to unpack and air out these passed-down loads of laundry.

Weeks later once we were down a shed full of boxes with my limbs reattached, I tell her I don't recognize this new person I'm becoming and it scares me. That I'm terrified of becoming my mother. That I didn't know I was carrying baggage and I'm not used to being so light. I tell her about my complicated views on "family". I share how I can't reconcile family with blood in most ways. I ask why my parents, in tandem of hurting each other, also chose to hurt me: the one who didn't choose to be here.

"What if their only job was to get you here?". I'm puzzled. "Go with me. What if their only assignment was to get you here, to *this* earth at *that* time, to be who you are and who you're destined to be, and you were never meant to have a relationship? It's natural to expect that: they're mom and dad. But sometimes 'mom and dad' aren't who we think they are. Sometimes they come along later as people who enter our lives and fill those gaps. And that's okay."

I never knew that was possible. And it made all the sense in the world. I sat in her chair speechless. She reminds me to breathe. I can't say anything.

"You mean I can let go? I can be okay?"

"Let them go, Joi. It's okay".

She has given me so many gems, including these quotes:
"My no is my no"
"Get out of the slave thinking, brown girl."
"Just breathe... and shut up."

And I gave myself this: "Yo, shoutout to me."

Being a Black woman in therapy[12] is now being normalized. Speaking openly and courageously about our individual and collective struggles is a revolutionary act. Us desiring and working towards being well is offensive and I, for one, no longer apologize for cherishing my livelihood over family secrets. I am no one's punching bag, waiting room or infirmary. I am not a harborer of unnecessary pain, a workhouse for the Black community, a willing participant in struggle love that never gets past struggle. In therapy, I speak of my dreams, my visions, being an empath, feeling everything. I completed an exercise that included naming everyone whose baggage I was still carrying. I wrote about my grandmother and feeling like her life, her baggage, is more of a mission for me. Again, I've cried and watched her cry. We've laughed together and talked shit. I wish I could bottle the purity of our first meeting and give it to every Black woman who doesn't feel seen. If it's any consolation, I see you, sis. And I'm proud of us.

I will continue to speak on the inside of therapy looking outward. More specifically, a Black woman on the inside of therapy looking out into the world with boxes full of losses and torn relationships asking - daring - to see the other side. It sounds like such a familiar tune that you believe you know where it's going. But that's the thing

---

12 "Therapy For Black Girls." https://www.therapyforblackgirls.com/. Accessed 30 Oct. 2019.

about tales that sound like old hat: they draw you in with new lessons beneath the seams. The familiarity hides the gold. I wish to keep speaking on being ripped from death's arms even as wanting to die was a brighter light than the actual sun. Would I have been just another statistic? Would it have been another case of a workhorse being laid to rest? The stakes are high as more stories of regret and turmoil seek happy endings. My story starts off bleak, as most hero's journeys do. But as the tears dry and the sun again hits my face with fresh breath in my lungs, I reach the other side with a woman who looks like me.

Some words on having your best therapy experience

#1. Bring it all with you. If anyone is equipped to handle all you have to say, it's a licensed clinician/psychologist/psychiatrist. It's literally their job. So please don't feel like you must keep anything to yourself. The right clinician will show you the lessons behind the trauma, not place blame on you and your reactions. Being emotionally honest and vulnerable will take you so far in reclaiming your mind after/during trauma.

#2. There's some shopping around to do. It's rare to luck out on the perfect therapist on your first time around the couch. The therapist I have now took six spins on the psychoanalysis wheel to find. I've been in therapy on and off for over 13 years. Some clinicians started off as good fits but gradually became less good. Some were judgey, some were heavily indoctrinated in religious ideology. It took time, which I understand can be difficult to digest. Treat finding a good therapist like choosing the best person to talk to in a spiral. You wouldn't (I hope) unload on just anybody. Take the time necessary to find the right person who will affirm, assess and, when necessary, collect you.

#3. It's okay to break up. One of the most beautiful things about meeting my current therapist is how accepting my old therapist was with me leaving. I had to break it to her that I found a therapist that could meet my needs as a Black woman, someone leaving the Christian religion and venturing into my roots with Hoodoo, someone with a differing language and coding. She understood and wished me well on my journey. With all the awful romantic breakups I've had, this breakup reaction came as a wonderful surprise. My past therapist gave me gems I still use today. I'm grateful for the time she took with me and her understanding that I needed something more. Breaking up with a therapist - or anyone for that matter - is never easy. There may be tears and feelings of rejection from both parties. But I challenge you to put your mental needs first over the needs of others.

How to be by your Black ass self

I sat in front of a reader who told me I was in mourning. I thought back on any people I knew who had transitioned recently and no one came to mind. I wondered if I was still bleeding from my grandmother and father dying two months apart the same year, after I pleaded with Heaven to let them live. I couldn't pull from where they were gathering my mourning. Then they said it didn't need to be actual death; it could be mourning people who were no longer with me on my journey. And right there it clicked. I've lost many friends in the last 5 years, and they each left my life when I chose to center myself. I've had one say I can "drink bleach and die," one who publicly mocked my efforts to bring together a community during yet another police shooting while I served as a key person on their team, two from high school who required I drop everything for them while being the only single mother in the crew. One while in the midst of one of the darkest times of my life basically asked, "but what about me?"

Sitting across from this reader, I began to feel my eyes swell. "Is this what this pain has been?", I asked myself. For most of that spring I had a weight on my chest I couldn't explain. It weighed me down; dropping me past mourning into despair. It was familiar and heavy. It wouldn't leave me until it was recognized. "You have to grieve," said the reader picking up on my short breaths. I thought I was fine. Many of these people left in the blazes of glory they intended - subliminal posts, snide comments, a rolling list of all the ways I'd failed them. And I would eat it. Consuming my ills as a bad friend.

I made it a pastime for people to treat me like shit. Times where their actions went unchecked by me, too afraid to present running records of their abuses of power and my wounds of kindness. I always pulled the most out of me to be the best friend I could be. As a kid, I was a walking library - bookbag full of books for all my friends to read. Once at recess, they all came over at the same time demanding their books. This one wasn't finished which pissed off the other waiting for that book. One folded the corners when I asked them not to. One asked when was I getting more books. Overheated and literally bent 90 degrees, I flung my bag full of books to the ground, books landing in a thud. "HERE!", I screamed while some teachers snapped from grown folk conversations to see the commotion. I stood there near tears with a scowl as each friend grabbed "their" book and quietly walked away. That should've tipped me off on how the path I was heading down wasn't healthy for me.

As I write this essay, I spend most of my time alone. I've become more comfortable with the way my voice sounds saying no. Leaving a party, event, space that makes me feel agitated is now easier. Picking up on the influx of anxiety triggered by being around people who cause me unrest doesn't so easily ring as mind games anymore. I've become intensely protective of my space, ears, sanity, vibes and internal frequency. Tryouts for the Projection Olympics are done. No matter of struggle for the sake of camaraderie seems useful. This isn't to say I will not walk with you through a struggle; it means I refuse to string myself as the bridge.

I've conducted a deep investigation into what makes up all of me. I've owned up to my shit and have since refused to take on anyone else's. I've stopped protecting those who would see me harmed. I've found my voice. It used to shake but, now, it vibrates. Courage has become synonymous with my name. And I've learned the invaluable lesson that everyone does not deserve the luxury of being my friend.

Some words on learning to love being alone

#1. Cherishing your own company is the best revenge.
Some people will abandon you just to see if you can float
on without them. Float. Ride every wave, sib. Emotional
dependence on others will leave you stranded every time.
I guarantee your sea legs are stronger than you think. So
strike out alone, doing all the things you want to do. Drag
your feet. Take your time. Drink in every single moment
you've been rushed by previously. Get to know how your
feet hit the ground on an intimate level, enjoying your
own pace.

#2. Be mindful.
Sometimes, being alone is all we can control. Taking a
moment to be alone even if you share a bed goes really
far. Reconnect with your body through breath. Find your
center before your feet hit the ground. Bring yourself to
this present moment. Control your breathing, your muscle
tensing, your thoughts as best you can. Control what you
can for that moment. Then prepare to greet the day.

#3. Do the things others won't.
My brother Jemeil is the ONLY person who loves derping
around any given city solely for the sake of it as much as I
do. We both appreciate art and spectacle; walking around
eating gelato because we can. That's one of my healing
activities- wandering. No real destination, just a time
when I am the captain without anyone else's input. I
learned how precious this is to me the hard way. For many
years, planning my birthday was an agonizing experience.

What made it so was other peoples' expectations of what I should do. Given the age, the landmark, the milestone, I'm *supposed* to do *this*. After many failed attempts with a few people hijacking my day, I stood firm on how much it means to me to be alone. I'm not sad or a person to which you must send pity. I'm a wanderer, eating gelato, taking in yet another museum. On my terms. All alone. And loving it.

How I got to know this woman

I'm running towards the gate where she stood. She looked like me, only with less light in her eyes. Throughout this journey, I assumed the final boss would be some amalgamation of every terroristic person in my life. Some strands of all my exes, my parents, overall shitty people who sought to break me because their lives are in shambles. I never thought in all my fighting, the final boss would be me.

I meet her at the gate - the gate she's guarding me from entering. She tells me it's not safe beyond the threshold. That staying here, with what's familiar - destructive yet familiar, is the safer option. I try to look her in the eyes. She refuses me. I stand there in technicolor while she languishes in dull tones of gray. I tell her I need her to move. "I can't stay here", I say. She decides to meet my eyes. She sees a version of herself staring back, glazed over with remnants of what used to be freedom. She mourns how she got here, but rejoices that this version of her is marching forward. She knows she can't last here. The moment I find freedom would mean the end of her. There is nothing left to guard, nothing left to protect. She knows this. Death is imminent. The gate begins to crumble. As I make one more wordless and impassioned plea, she breaks her gaze. She reaches her arm towards the latch. She pulls back the door. I thank her. She shields herself from me as she fades into ashes. I walk into the new.

I know more boss battles await me in the future, and with every victory and defeat, I learn even more about my fortitude. I don't fully know what lies ahead for me. With every step, I grow more confident that I've made the right choices now. I've learned to honor my gut. I've learned the ins and outs of my intuition. I've learned there is, in fact, resiliency in trauma[13].

I've been unfolding. I'm still unfolding.

I keep telling myself that I have more pages to fill. As lessons become new habits, broken skin begins to heal, the knowledge gained must be documented. It must be shared.

How do we share?
By telling the stories, over whiskey.

---

[13] "My Food History Wasn't Lost. It Was Stolen. - The Sporkful." 4 Nov. 2019, http://www.sporkful.com/my-food-history-wasnt-lost-it-was-stolen/. Accessed 18 Nov. 2019.

About the Author

Joi Donaldson writes from the heart. She is a 10x published author, an accomplished poet, professional photographer and all-around storytelling badass. She has bylines with Midnight & Indigo, xoNecole, Raising Mothers, Richmond Magazine just to name a few. She's a curator of good vibes and, through transparency and humor, has learned how to make tough conversations fun through her podcast with Montrell White called My Depression's Got Jokes. Check out her work:

Website: www.joiunspeakable.com
Portfolio: www.rightsidereign.pixieset.com

Medium: medium.com/@joi_unspeakable

Joi is a mother, storyteller, advocate and survivor
currently calling Maryland home.

www.ingramcontent.com/pod-product-compliance
Lightning Source LLC
Chambersburg PA
CBHW021236090426
42740CB00006B/558